R.S.V.P.—A DYNAMIC APPROACH TO STUDY

68-7900

THOMAS STATON

Huntingdon College

R.S.V.P.

A DYNAMIC APPROACH TO STUDY

SCOTT, FORESMAN AND COMPANY

Illustrations by John Everds

Library of Congress Catalog Card No. 66-14844
Copyright © 1966 by Scott, Foresman and Company, Glenview, Illinois 60025
All Rights Reserved. Printed in the United States of America.
Regional offices of Scott, Foresman and Company are located
in Atlanta, Dallas, Glenview, Palo Alto, and Oakland, N.J.

CONTENTS

PLANNING
YOUR
COLLEGE CAREER

Why did you come to college?

This is not intended as a hypothetical question. Why *did* you come? Your real, honest purpose in coming to college should determine how you spend your time here. Your reasons for entering college should determine the relative importance you place on the different activities that constantly demand a college student's time and effort.

Every year thousands of people enter college for any of five different reasons. These reasons differ widely in the motivation they afford and greatly affect the probable amount and type of effort these people will expend in college. People may come to college:

1. To acquire knowledge and skills that will be helpful in building a successful career

2. Because it is the socially approved thing to do and a college degree is a useful status symbol

3. To postpone having to go to work

4. To get a husband

5. For fun, football, friends, and frivolity

If you came to college for the first reason given—to learn things that will help you be a more successful person during the remainder of your life—this book will help you. Following its suggestions will not place a greater demand on your time than is reasonable and necessary, and by spending your study time in the way proposed here, you can gain the most possible learning from the time spent.

If you came for any of the other four reasons given, or perhaps for some reason not listed here, working at your studies with the thoroughness suggested in this book may interfere with other activities you have in mind and to which you attach high importance. However, following the study plan given here will increase your chances of passing and thus of remaining in college until your real objective has been achieved or altered.

Before beginning to study this book, complete the college career planning charts on the following pages. The purpose of doing this is to help you to (1) identify precisely your *real* reasons for attending college, (2) accurately evaluate your present academic skills and abilities, and (3) plan your college days in the light of your aims and needs. The more honest and accurate you are in following the planning sequence set out here, the better your chance of designing a program to fit your own particular situation.

PLANNING CHARTS

I. How important in your decision to attend college was each of the reasons given below? After each, write the per cent you believe best approximates its importance compared with the others. Be as honest and as discerning of your motives as possible because such an analysis of your own true motives will help you. The sum of your figures should be 100.

Reasons I Am Attending College

To gain knowledge and/or skills needed in a career   _____%

Because attending college and/or getting a degree is the "proper" thing for one of my group to do (coming because parents insisted on it falls here)   _____%

To postpone going to work   _____%

To get a husband   _____%

For a good time—fun, friends, football, and frivolity   _____%

Other reasons (specify) _____   _____%
_____   _____%

100 %

Adam, Betty, Connie, Dale, and Earl are among the thirty members of their graduating class at Canton High School who went to State University in the fall. Once there, their patterns of life differed considerably. As you read the following thumbnail sketches of their backgrounds, plans, hopes, and beliefs, determine which of the five common motives or combination of motives for attending college was dominant in each of them. To what extent do your own motives resemble the apparent motives of each of them?

Adam does not know what he wants to do in life, but figures that a liberal arts degree will constitute a good foundation for whatever it may be. He is considering several areas as possible majors—English, economics, or psychology. He thinks any one of these would be a definite asset in almost any vocation and hopes he can take at least a couple of courses in each before he has to make a final decision about his major and minor. He has an idea he will end up majoring in the department in which he makes best grades on his introductory courses, because he knows major professors often are consulted by potential employers of college graduates, and he feels this would be a good way of getting a good recommendation.

It would appear that Adam's purpose in attending college is:

Betty has little interest in the academic side of college, but she diligently works to keep her grades at a respectable level. She plans to major in sociology, feeling that this field will give her a better-than-average knowledge of society and social dynamics. She dreams of a home in the suburbs and the pleasant life of a young matron in the midst of friends she has known since childhood, and of belonging to clubs and taking part in the civic and social activities of the other young women of her set.

Betty's hopes and plans suggest that her motivation to attend college grows out of:

Connie went to Canton High on a school bus each day from the outlying rural area where her father owned and operated a dairy farm. If she had not gone to college, she would have had to choose between helping her parents on the farm or taking the type of job open to a high school graduate in some nearby town or city. Neither appealed to her. She does not plan to be a "career woman." She expects to get married and find her life satisfaction in being a wife and mother, making a good home for her family. She is a conscientious student and tries to have a well-rounded college life of study and social activities, and still earn part of her expenses by working in the registrar's office.

Connie's probable reasons for attending college were:

Dale does just barely enough work to stay in college. He is not very active in extracurricular activities, but he has several rather close friends with whom he spends most of his time. He is vague about his plans for a major, but he figures it will work itself out somehow. Dale's father expects him to enter the family dry-cleaning business when he finishes at State. Dale is not very keen on this, but he doesn't know just what he does want to do. He hopes that attending college will open up some area of interest for him and get him on the road to a satisfactory vocation.

From the information given here, what would you suspect was Dale's real reason for coming to college?

Earl follows much the same pattern at State that he did in high school, where, in the Class Annual, his motto was recorded: "Never let schoolwork interfere with getting an education." He worries if he is in danger of failing a course, but seldom gives it a thought until just before a big test or examination. He is popular, is interested in every possible activity at State, and never has enough hours in the day to get everything done that he wants to do. He is mildly concerned about the prospect of earning a living when he gets out of college, but he figures that anyone who gets along with people as well as he does can make good at something and that he can successfully cross that bridge when he comes to it.

Earl probably came to college to:

II. Think back on your high school career—your study habits, your grades, the things that were hardest or easiest for you, and remarks made by your various teachers about your abilities. Indicate by number (1 for the skill in which you consider you

What Are Your Strong Points?

Where Do Your Skills Need Reinforcing?

are best, to 6 for that at which you are poorest) your *present* relative skill or ability in each of these six academic tasks.

Analysis of My Academic Skills

_____ reading

_____ understanding and profiting from lectures

_____ thinking and solving problems

_____ oral participation in the classroom

_____ writing (expressing your ideas, not penmanship)

_____ taking tests and examinations

How can your high school grades be explained in terms of your skills as they are rated above?

III. The typical college student has about ten hours per weekday, after sleeping, eating, attending classes, and necessary personal grooming, in which to do all the other things that demand his attention. Considering (1) your primary and secondary goals in attending college, (2) your relative skill in the six academic tasks, and (3) the demands of your various college courses, indicate below the number of hours per weekday you think you should devote to each activity that may demand your time and attention in college. (Do not consider the time from noon on Friday until noon Sunday in estimating hours. This much leeway is *always* needed for a college student to take care of inevitable but often unpredictable activities such as preparing a special report or taking his car to the garage for repairs.)

Allocation of My Time

_____ studying

_____ dating

_____ part-time job

_____ conversation, general "socializing," fraternity, sorority, or club activities

_____ physical exercise and athletics

_____ travel to and from college

_____ other (specify) _____

_____   _____

====

10 hours (approximate available hours per weekday to allocate)

IV. Having honestly considered and assessed your motives, your abilities and skills in academic areas, and a reasonable distribution of the unscheduled hours available, you should be able to construct a workable, reasonable time schedule to guide you. Use the chart on the following page to make yourself a weekly time schedule. Merely making it will help you, because it will focus your attention on time allocation as a means of making time available for all the activities in your life. But, of course, to get *high* value from the schedule, it must be a good, realistic one, and you must follow it fairly regularly. Being successful in college probably will require more careful and efficient use of your time than you have ever achieved before. A well thought out and faithfully followed schedule is your best assurance of achieving optimum utilization of your time.

Weekly Schedule of My Time							
Time	Sun.	Mon.	Tues.	Wed.	Thurs.	Fri.	Sat.
7:00							
8:00							
9:00							
10:00							
11:00							
12:00							
1:00							
2:00							
3:00							
4:00							
5:00							
6:00							
7:00							
8:00							
9:00							
10:00							
11:00							

HOW TO GET THE MOST FROM THIS BOOK

Chapter One

First   Examine the table of contents to see the outline of the book.

Second   Perform the self-analysis and planning exercises on pages 2-7.

Third   Read this chapter to find how and why learning how to study will help you.

Fourth   Study Chapter Two until you understand the use of the R.S.V.P. procedure; then use the system in studying the rest of this book.

Fifth   Make a habit of using the R.S.V.P. attack on each of your reading and listening tasks every day and use the applicable portions of it in your study tasks, as described in this book. This is the payoff. The more you practice the system, the more proficient you become, and the better and faster you will learn.

Sixth   When you are going to participate in classroom discussion, write papers, or take tests, review the pertinent sections of this book for guidance in doing the job most effectively.

[1]   Give ten normal children plenty of opportunity to play in a pool with water deep enough to swim in, and nine out of the ten eventually will learn to swim—after a fashion. Not one out of ten, however, will learn a method of swimming that will earn him a place on a good college swimming team. To meet collegiate competition, the self-taught swimmer would have to *un*-learn many things as well as learn many new and different techniques, movements, and procedures.

[2]   Studying is more complicated than swimming, and most "natural" methods of studying fall as far short of maximum effectiveness and efficiency as do "natural" methods of swimming. The crawl is a less natural stroke, and is harder to learn, than the dog paddle, but, once learned, it is a much more effective way of swimming. Similarly, few students accidentally hit on and perfect a highly efficient method of studying—they "dog-paddle," as it were, through their study assignments. Some develop some truly excellent learning skills, but few attain any-

thing like the level of study efficiency that is possible through using a carefully designed study procedure. Such a system, like the crawl, is more complicated to learn than the "natural" method, but it similarly gives better results when practiced and skillfully used.

3   Typing is another good example of a skill that may be self-taught. Touch typing, as contrasted with the hunt and peck system, is less "natural," to be sure, and more difficult to learn, but it gives results that are well worth the extra trouble. The R.S.V.P. system of study described in this book can be compared to the crawl or to the touch system of typing. It is more difficult to perfect than the average student's "natural" method of study, but it produces greater learning in less time.

4   This text is called *A Dynamic Approach to Study* because it emphasizes the *psychodynamics*—the fundamental psychological forces and mechanisms producing learning—and suggests study procedures that harness and use these forces. It is not concerned with tricks or gimmicks professing to produce learning without effort (they don't!), nor with general collegiate topics such as how to adjust to campus life. Instead, it explores the dynamics of learning, the forces and mechanisms that cause learning to take place, and the ways in which these dynamics can be applied and used in performing the academic tasks required of college students.

5   There are certain basic academic tasks required of almost all students. In practically all colleges, universities, and professional schools, students are required to (1) read assignments, (2) listen to lectures, (3) think, reason, and solve problems, (4) participate in classroom discussions, (5) write assigned papers, and (6) take examinations. Each of these academic tasks can profitably be considered a type of study, because each of them is a form of mental activity by which you learn.

6   You can see that these tasks fall into three broad categories: Reading and listening are processes by which you acquire information; thinking is the process through which you convert information into knowledge; and talking, writing, and taking examinations are processes by which your knowledge is applied or demonstrated. Taken together, these six types of study include most of the academic activities you will be expected to engage in during your college career. If you are able to accomplish them effectively, college should be a highly satisfying and successful experience for you.

7   From the chapters that follow, you will realize that learning is not something that occurs automatically as a result of your hearing or seeing something. Learning takes place as a result of your *mental reaction* to what you see or hear; this reaction is a major factor in the learning process. Learning generally occurs in

proportion to the intensity of your concentration on what you are to learn.

8 Despite what you may have heard to the contrary, you learn little by *doing*. You learn by *thinking about what you are doing*. You learn little by merely reading a book or by hearing a lecture. You learn by thinking about what you read or what you hear, by mentally reacting to it, by aggressively concentrating your thinking and reasoning powers on it, and thereby "figuring out" what it means and what its significance is. A good typist may make a dozen copies of a letter, each copy obviously requiring her to read her model and type it verbatim, but after the twelfth reading she may have only a vague idea of what she has read and typed. This is because, although she was conscious of the words she was reading and typing, she was not thinking about their meaning.

9 A few years ago there was quite a hullabaloo over "sleep learning." Using a tape recording of a lecture or a chapter from a book, one could, it was hoped, learn the material while he slept simply by setting the tape recorder to play the message over and over again beside his bed. This was indeed painless education, but it did not work. It did not work because a person

Good Grades Don't
Just Happen

They Are Produced!

GOOD — Study (review, study, verbalize, preview)

GOOD — Thinking

GOOD — Writing

GOOD — Reciting

GOOD — Test-Taking

= GOOD GRADES

does not learn while he is asleep. He does not learn while he is asleep because during sleep his mind does not concentrate on a subject—does not engage in sustained, intensive, purposeful thinking. And learning occurs very much in proportion to the amount of mental energy used—the concentrated, sustained, purposeful thinking that a person does. You will see when you study Chapter Two that the R.S.V.P. procedure of study requires a high level of concentrated, sustained, purposeful thinking. This system capitalizes on the psychological causes of learning, the psychodynamics of learning.

Robert had never thought much about the "scientific" way of doing things as compared to the "natural" way. He recognized at once, however, the advantage of the touch system of typing over the hunt and peck method, and of developing an efficient swimming stroke. After he read this chapter, he considered for the first time the possibility of a better way of studying than the "natural" way he always had gone about reading a textbook. He asked himself some questions about the difference between his usual method of studying and the way he was advised to begin studying this book.

1. What does this chapter advise me to do in beginning to study a book that most people usually have *not* done?

2. What are the possible advantages of doing this?

You Will Improve the Effectiveness of Your Study Very Little Like This

But a Lot Like This!

THE R.S.V.P.
PROCEDURE
OF STUDY

Chapter Two

1 REVIEW what led up to your present assignment;
then
STUDY* it by carefully reading it (or listening to it);
then
VERBALIZE it, *i.e.*, write or say it in your own words;
then
PREVIEW what is coming next.

2 R.S.V.P. on an invitation you receive means that you are asked not merely to look at the invitation but to respond to it. A college, when you get right down to it, can only issue to its students invitations to learn. It can extend to you the opportunity to learn, but for you to take advantage of this invitation, you must respond to it, you must "R.S.V.P." In this book R.S.V.P. also stands for the four steps given above—steps by which you can respond effectively and efficiently to an invitation to learn. Whenever you study an assignment, follow these four steps to learn the assignment much more thoroughly than you would by using your own "natural" method of study. For maximum effectiveness of your study, in each study period go through them in the order shown—R.S.V.P.

3 The steps for which R.S.V.P. stands in this book are REVIEW, STUDY, VERBALIZE, and PREVIEW. Using the R.S.V.P. attack on each study task to which it is applicable, as will be described in the following chapters, will bring into play many of the psychological factors that promote effective learning. The R.S.V.P. steps constitute a dynamic approach to study: Performing them stimulates your mind to work at a study task in an active, imaginative manner that maximizes your learning.

4 Let us examine each step in detail to see the purpose it serves and how you can go through it in your daily study periods. For purposes of illustration, we shall assume that your class meets daily. When you follow the R.S.V.P. procedure, your daily study periods will run as follows:

---

* In this book, the word *study* will be used in the usual sense; it also will be used to designate one particular step in the R.S.V.P. procedure, the step of *reading* or *listening*. When used to refer to the STUDY step in the R.S.V.P. procedure, the word will appear as in this sentence.

Evening, October 1

1. REVIEW what you covered in class today, October 1.
2. STUDY the assignment for the next class meeting, October 2. (You will have PREVIEWED this material at the end of yesterday's study period, September 30.)
3. VERBALIZE the material after you STUDY it.
4. PREVIEW the material you expect to be assigned for the day after tomorrow, October 3.

Evening, October 2

1. REVIEW the material that you STUDIED and VERBALIZED last night, which was covered in the classroom today, October 2.
2. STUDY the assignment for tomorrow, October 3, which you PREVIEWED last night.
3. VERBALIZE what you have just STUDIED for tomorrow's class.
4. PREVIEW what you expect to be assigned for the day after tomorrow, October 4.

⁵ You will readily see from this schedule of typical study periods that the first thing you will do in each day's study period is to REVIEW the material covered in class that same morning (or afternoon). This brings you up to the assignment for tomorrow. Having the topic of today's classroom lecture or discussion fresh in your mind will give you a clearer view of the material assigned for you to study for tomorrow's class. You will also see from the schedule given here that your *first* acquaintance with any assignment is gained through PREVIEWING that assignment; you will have done this during the final minutes of your previous study session. Since what you gain from this brief PREVIEW of an assignment will be essential to your most effective STUDY of it, let us consider this PREVIEW step first.

Preview

⁶ You know how much easier it is to put a jigsaw puzzle together if you have previously examined the completed picture carefully and know exactly how the picture is supposed to look when you have finished it. Through previewing the puzzle you have learned what sort of picture you are trying to construct, what you are working toward. As a result, you are able to work

with greater speed and accuracy in putting it together. PREVIEW-ING material that you are preparing to study in detail serves the same general purpose as looking at the picture you are going to complete from the jigsaw puzzle pieces. It gives you a good idea of the overall scheme or pattern of the subject, and as a result you can study the individual topics and ideas with greater comprehension because you know the general form of the subject of which they are parts. This is why you were asked to study the table of contents of this book before proceeding beyond the first page. Doing so gave you a PREVIEW of the overall organization and nature of what you later will study. You should do this with each new text you are to study: Examine the table of contents to get an idea of the overall scope and organization of the book. Also, if the table of contents breaks down each chapter into subtopics, as does the table of contents of this book, you will find it helpful to refer to it as you proceed through the book, reviewing the organization of each new chapter as you prepare to study it.

7 There are several ways to PREVIEW an assignment. The quickest method is to turn to the table of contents and examine the titles of subsections of the chapter you are studying. This will give you a sketchy overall picture of what the chapter will contain, but the listing of topics given in a table of contents seldom is detailed enough to give you a thorough PREVIEW of the chapter.

8 Some authors begin each chapter with a foreword or an outline briefly telling what the chapter is about. (Paragraph 1 of this chapter provides such an outline.) Some authors end each chapter with a summary. Whenever you begin to study a text, check the author's plan. Find out whether he begins a chapter with an outline or a paragraph giving a general idea of what the chapter includes. Check the end of the chapter to see if he finishes with a summary. If he has included either of these study helps, begin your study of the chapter by a careful reading of the outline, the preview paragraph, or the summary.

9 At first it may seem a little awkward to begin the study of a chapter by reading its summary. You probably have been accustomed throughout life to thinking of the summary as something you read when you have finished the chapter (if, indeed, you read it at all!). However, it will be of more benefit as an introduction to the chapter than as a conclusion. You will find that a great many psychology textbooks contain summaries at the end of chapters, and many contain previews. Psychologists have recognized how valuable to a student these short condensations of the material discussed in greater detail in the chapter can be.

10 Whenever your text does not have one of these helps to familiarize you with the material you are to study, you will need

to use the device called "scanning." Scanning is simply running your eyes rapidly down a page, picking up an idea from each paragraph to get the general theme, the "drift," of the author. When scanning, you do not read complete paragraphs. Frequently, you will not even read complete sentences. Your eyes will race down the page picking up a phrase here, a clause there—just enough to get a picture of what it is the author is talking about, not what he is saying about it. Scanning is done so rapidly that you will spend only four or five minutes in scanning a complete assignment if you are proceeding at the rate this PREVIEW step expects of you. If you are spending more than fifteen to thirty seconds per page, you probably are reading in too much detail and need to teach yourself to speed more rapidly down the paragraphs, looking at each one only long enough to get the general idea of what it is about. As you may gather, good scanning is hard mental work. You cannot let your eyes languidly drift down the page and your mind foggily ramble along. Your eyes are literally racing down the page, and your mind is working at top speed and power trying to glean rapidly and accurately the import of the words that your eyes are picking up.

¹¹   Here is a test by which you can tell whether your scanning has been effective. When you finish PREVIEWING a chapter or a shorter portion of material by the scanning method, pause and ask yourself, "What was the general idea of this material I have been scanning?" Write a brief summary—one short paragraph—expressing either the *scope* or the *main point* of what you have read. It is important that, at least for a few days, you *write* your summary rather than merely say it to yourself; the discipline of putting the general impression of what you have read into concrete, recorded words will show you how well or how poorly you identified the substance of what you PREVIEWED and will thus suggest how to improve the quality of your subsequent PREVIEWS. At the end of each chapter of this book, beginning with Chapter Three, space will be provided for you to write a summary paragraph identifying the scope of the chapter or the main topics covered in it, after you have PREVIEWED it. Be sure to do this; it is your surest means of ensuring that you are scanning (PREVIEWING) effectively. It is because *you* are to scan the chapter and then write this paragraph that the author has not provided in this book the PREVIEW aids mentioned in paragraphs 8 and 9—a foreword or outline at the beginning of each chapter or a summary paragraph at the end.

¹²   If you find that you can form a relatively clear idea of what the topic was about, probably you have scanned the material effectively. If, on the other hand, you cannot reconstruct the general pattern of the material you have scanned, you need to go over it again, perhaps a little more slowly, or, more probably,

with your mind working harder at translating the words your eyes pick up into an outline. With an effective PREVIEW, you will be able to grasp more effectively the details of what you subsequently STUDY, and to integrate them into a more meaningful overall understanding of the topic.

Study

13   *Think* about what you are studying as you read an assignment—*go after the meaning.* This is the biggest secret of effective studying. Throughout the remainder of this section we will discuss ways in which you can train yourself to think effectively about what you are studying. All the suggestions given will be aimed at this one objective: to get you to think effectively about what you are reading.

14   Stop for a minute right now and think about what this means. It means that as you read an assignment you should not merely read and try to mentally take in each word, but you must deliberately look for the meaning of sentences. You should try to understand what the author is saying and perceive the significance and implications of his material. Effective study is not done with the eyes alone. All the eyes can do is pick up words from the printed page. Then your mind has to take over. You must take those words, interpret them, occasionally use a dictionary to clarify new or unfamiliar words, get the significance of them, and make them form in your thoughts the sense of what the author is saying. If you depend only on your eyes in your studying, at best you will retain a foggy memory of what you read, without any real understanding of it; at worst you will do what all of us have done many times—read a complete paragraph or chapter without having gained a glimmer of an idea of what the author was really getting at.

15   Here, in a nutshell, is the way to approach the STUDY step of the R.S.V.P. procedure effectively: When you start to STUDY an assignment, pick up a pencil. Read a paragraph. Then pause to think about the contents of the paragraph. Boil down what it said into the fewest words that you possibly can, and write those words in the margin of your text. If you are unable to summarize a paragraph after reading it, you have not fully comprehended its meaning. In this case, it is worse than useless to go on to the next paragraph. Instead, while the first reading of the paragraph is fresh in your mind, go over it again, this time with added effort to grasp the real significance of the words that the author has written.

16   After you have studied a few assignments in this manner— that is, reading a paragraph, striving to get the main idea of it, then making a brief marginal note of the main idea—you will

find that as a matter of habit you will begin to read for real understanding. No longer will you be reading a paragraph with your mind vaguely wandering around somewhere up in the clouds, with the result that when you have read the paragraph you have no idea what it says. All of us tend to lapse into this lazy habit at times, but reading with a pencil in your hand, constantly reminding you that as soon as you finish reading the paragraph you must make yourself summarize what it says, rather quickly breaks you of the habit of reading only with your eyes while your mind is taking a vacation.

17   It is important that you actually *write* your summary of the paragraph in the margin of your book. This serves several purposes. In the first place, writing it in the margin of the book keeps you from simply copying down the entire mass of words and thereby successfully evading thinking through to an understanding of the paragraph. To fit your notes into the margin space available, you are forced into thinking clearly and concisely to the main point of the author's paragraph. Furthermore, the notes that you have written beside each paragraph will be invaluable aids in performing the REVIEW step of the R.S.V.P. plan for daily study, and also in reviewing for tests and examinations. Finally, no matter how conscientious you intend to be, unless you know you have to write down that succinct condensation, you will tend to think, "Oh yes, . . . well . . . I understand *that!*" and pass on to the next paragraph without really crystallizing your vague idea of what the paragraph meant. So STUDY with your pencil in your hand, and write your own digest of the substance of each paragraph in the margin beside it. Your book may not look pretty, but to STUDY in this way virtually guarantees high concentration and vast improvement in your comprehension of the material you study.

18   *Begin to do this now.* From this point on, throughout the book, make a brief summary note beside each paragraph. The wide margins were especially provided to give you plenty of room for your notes, and the number beside each paragraph is to make it easy to locate a specific paragraph which might be brought up for discussion in class. By the time you have completed this book, you should have become quite skillful in identifying the gist of a paragraph and expressing it in a few well-selected words.

Verbalize

19   One dictionary definition of the word *verbalize* is "to express oneself or something precisely, skillfully . . . ." When you VERBALIZE what you have read, you are, in effect, reciting your lesson orally to yourself rather than in a classroom before

the instructor and other students. Recitation implies presenting in your own words material that has been prepared earlier. In the R.S.V.P. study procedure, you VERBALIZE in your own words the precise thought of a paragraph. You have partially accomplished this step in performing the STUDY step described above, for you verbalize when you condense the author's paragraphs into a few words that sum up the essence of his thoughts. However, as a separate and distinct step in the R.S.V.P. system of study, VERBALIZING involves considerably more than summarizing the paragraph in the fewest possible words, as in the STUDY step. This is only a starting point for the full procedure of VERBALIZING.

20   The complete VERBALIZING step can be performed immediately after reading each paragraph, but you may find it more effective to STUDY your complete assignment and then go over it again to perform the VERBALIZING step. Let us assume, therefore, that you have now STUDIED an entire assignment, which, you remember, you have PREVIEWED earlier. As you STUDIED it, you made penciled summaries of each paragraph in the margin. Now turn back to the beginning of the assignment. Read the note that you wrote in the margin beside the first paragraph. Now state as completely as you can the entire thought of this paragraph. Your marginal note stated the thought you decided was the *main* idea of the paragraph, but the paragraph may also contain several other important ideas. Do you see how this differs from the succinct writing you did in the STUDY step? Then you were trying to get just the barest, briefest outline of what was said in the paragraph. Now, in the VERBALIZING step, you are trying to say in your own words, as completely and thoroughly as possible, all that the author said.

21   When you have finished VERBALIZING the paragraph, glance at the paragraph in the book to see if you omitted any important elements. If you did, they probably will now stick in your mind so that you will remember them in the future. If you did not omit anything important, you have a clear understanding of that paragraph and are ready to go on to the next one. Repeat this procedure for each paragraph: Look at your penciled note to remind yourself of the topic the paragraph is about, then say as completely as possible all the thoughts, ideas, and facts that the author included in the paragraph, then check your VERBALIZING against the text itself.

22   This may sound to you like a rather formidable job, but by the time you have done a dozen paragraphs, VERBALIZING each one fully, you will begin to master the technique. By the time you have studied a half-dozen or so assignments in this manner, you will be performing the VERBALIZING step as a natural follow-up to reading the material, and you will find that you are *learning*

verbalize = putting precise thought of paragraph in your own words your assignments with a thoroughness that you probably never achieved before. Careful experiments have shown that VERBAL-IZING material you have read contributes more to your learning of the material than rereading it does. In fact, for college students who read at an average rate of speed, it has been found that spending a third to a half of one's study time on the VERBALIZING step usually produces a greater amount of learning than spending a higher proportion on the reading step.

23 If you are a fast reader, covering material faster than the average college student, experiments have shown that *you* may find it most profitable to spend half or even more of your total study time in VERBALIZING the material you have read. This would mean spending one half or less of your time in the actual reading, and one half or more of your time in stating in your own words the real significance of what you read. This may be a new idea to you, but it is not a new idea in educational psychology. Thousands of students have found the principle to hold good in their own study. In addition, controlled experiments in psychological laboratories have shown that spending a large proportion of total study time in VERBALIZING what had been read produced better memory and understanding of the material than spending the same amount of time in rereading it.

24 At least at the beginning of your practice in using the R.S.V.P. system of daily study, you should do your VERBALIZING aloud—that is, actually say in your normal speaking voice the substance of each paragraph you have read. If you are studying in the library or in a room with other people, understandably they may not be enthusiastic about your speaking out periodically in your normal speaking voice, telling what you have just read. In this situation, however, you should be sure that you move your lips and form the distinct, precise words that summarize what you have read. As you become expert at VERBALIZING, you may find it sufficient merely to think over in your mind the substance of the paragraph, but it is dangerous to depend on that, especially before you have become proficient in VERBALIZING. Why is it dangerous? Because, human nature being what it is, you will tend to think lightly and fleetingly about what you have just read and will fool yourself into mistaking a vague, nebulous, foggy impression of what the paragraph is about for a thorough, lucid knowledge and understanding of it.

25 All of us have had the experience of having what we thought was an excellent idea, a marvelous understanding or comprehension of something, and, when we started to put the beautiful idea or understanding into words, finding that it slipped away from us, as when we might try to grasp a handful of fog or smoke. The first few times you attempt the VERBALIZING step, you may find this occasionally happening to you. Unless

you actually attempt to put your thoughts into precise words, you will not really know whether or not you have thought through the paragraph to the point of thoroughly comprehending it. Even after you have become quite skillful in using the R.S.V.P. method of studying, it is well occasionally to check your progress by saying aloud the substance of the paragraph you have just read to make sure that you have not slipped back into the easy habit of mistaking a vague impression of what a paragraph was about for a clear, lucid, precise understanding of it.

Review

26   Psychological experiments have shown that reviewing material which has been studied, thus refreshing and renewing it in your mind, causes the material to fade out much less rapidly than if it had not been reviewed. You begin to forget anything that you have studied immediately after you cease studying it. After a few hours, you have forgotten a good many of the details that were clear in your mind immediately following your study of a topic. At this crucial point, somewhere between six and twenty-four hours after studying a subject, carefully review that subject. Not only will you refresh the material in your mind, but after reinforcing your memory by review, you will forget much more slowly and not nearly as much as you would had you not performed this review.

27   What is the most effective way of REVIEWING? As you may have guessed, it is not rereading the material that you have previously studied. Most effective REVIEWING consists of forcing yourself to recall all the previously studied material that you can remember, then briefly scanning the textbook to see if your memory omitted anything important. Here again the penciled notes that you made in the margins of your book are very helpful. They simplify your REVIEW. You look at the note beside the paragraph, then attempt to elaborate what the paragraph said, exactly as you did in the VERBALIZE step. REVIEWING is actually a repeat performance of the VERBALIZE step, but it is done at a later period rather than immediately after reading an assignment. You will not, of course, be able to recall as many details from the text in your REVIEWING as you did in the original VERBALIZING. But after reading your penciled notes and attempting to VERBALIZE the contents of the paragraph as fully as possible, use the scanning technique to see if you missed any important points, and, if so, to refresh your mind with the things you did not remember.

28   Actually, after a classroom hour on an assignment, you should have an even better idea of relationships, important facts, overall concepts, and so on, than at the time of your original study of the material. Do not slight the REVIEW step in your

studying. Investing a comparatively small amount of time in REVIEWING the last assignment that you covered in class before going on to your new assignment will repay you handsomely. It will get your mind centered on the subject and will lead you up to tomorrow's assignment. It also will refresh your memory, and your memory will then continue at a higher level than it would have maintained without the REVIEW.

R.S.V.P. Applied to This Book

29 There you have the R.S.V.P. system of study. It is an invitation to learn, and if you will respond, you should greatly improve the efficiency and effectiveness of your study. Now use the R.S.V.P. technique in studying the next chapter of this book. PREVIEW Chapter Three right now, before you lay your book aside. Glance at the table of contents to see the plan of the chapter, scan the chapter to get the general theme, and write a short paragraph summarizing the main ideas. When you finish your PREVIEW, either take a rest period or wait until tomorrow before STUDYING Chapter Three thoroughly, as you normally would do in preparing assignments by the R.S.V.P. method. (We will assume in our discussion here that you are going to wait until tomorrow before STUDYING it.)

30 When you pick this book up (tomorrow) to STUDY Chapter Three in detail, use the R.S.V.P. procedure of daily study. First of all, REVIEW Chapter Two (today's lesson). Next, carefully STUDY Chapter Three with your pencil in hand, making marginal notes beside each paragraph as we described under the STUDY step. You may find that you can read the chapter with greater ease, speed, and comprehension than you have been accustomed to, because your PREVIEW of the chapter makes it easier for you to read faster and with higher comprehension. See if the summary paragraph you wrote after PREVIEWING Chapter Three seems adequate to you now, after STUDYING the assignment in detail.

31 Having read Chapter Three and written marginal notes of the gist of the paragraphs, turn back to the beginning of the chapter, glance at your note written beside the first paragraph, and say aloud in your own words, as completely as possible, all that paragraph contained. Then scan the paragraph to see if you remembered it accurately and completely. Go through the entire chapter in this way, paragraph by paragraph. Remember, the time spent VERBALIZING will give you bigger returns in learning than rereading the chapter would, for this is *thinking*, and we learn by thinking about what we read, not by the act of reading. Then, before you lay this book aside, PREVIEW Chapter Four. When you have done this, you will have completed an

assignment using the R.S.V.P. system. Expect to know this material much more thoroughly than you customarily know material you have studied. You will not be disappointed, because you have followed a series of steps that give you the greatest possible learning, understanding, and retention for the time you expend in study.

32 The R.S.V.P. method is not a gimmick, a mental trick that produces an illusion of learning. It works, produces a real improvement in your rate and quality of learning, because it is solidly based on proven psychological principles related to learning. Trying to remember a dozen or so psychological principles and trying to apply all of them at the same time as you listen, write, or accomplish one of the other study tasks would be too complicated. What you need for highly efficient study is a system which, if followed, enables you to bring the psychological principles promoting learning into play almost automatically. This is what the R.S.V.P. procedure of study is designed to do.

33 In Chapter Three we will examine some of the psychological factors that influence how much you learn and remember when you study a subject, and see how the R.S.V.P. procedure helps you to capitalize on the various factors. PREVIEW it now and write your short summary of the chapter on page 42.

Sarah took one look at the R.S.V.P. study procedure and decided it was not for her. When urged to try it, she gave her reasons for immediately rejecting it. "In the first place," she said, "I have to read and write reports on six novels this semester. If I studied twenty-four hours a day, seven days a week, I couldn't get through them using the R.S.V.P. method. In the second place, I don't have time to make notes; I'm a slow reader. In the third place, that VERBALIZE step is of no use to me. I want to *learn* an assignment, not *talk about* it, and anyway, I'm no good at talking about a topic I've read in a textbook. I *know* it all right, but I just can't express it in words."

1. Evaluate Sarah's objection that she has too much assigned reading to use the R.S.V.P. study procedure.

2. Should a slow reader take time to make notes of what he reads? Why or why not?

3. Evaluate Sarah's statement that she wants to learn, not talk about, an assignment.

4. What is the value of carrying out the VERBALIZE step if you are poor at expressing ideas in your own words?

PSYCHOLOGICAL FOUNDATIONS OF R.S.V.P.

Chapter Three

1   Most effective study requires not only skill in an efficient technique of study but also an understanding of the basic psychological factors that promote learning. The R.S.V.P. method of study was designed to capitalize on as many of the psychological facts that make for efficient learning as possible. However, you can capitalize on these factors most effectively if you know what they are—that is, if you know the psychological factors in learning that underlie each step of the R.S.V.P. procedure and the function that each step serves from the standpoint of the psychology of learning. The present chapter, therefore, will be devoted to an explanation of some psychological principles underlying effective learning and how the R.S.V.P. system of study exploits each one to maximize the effectiveness of your study.

2   There are no "laws" of learning in the sense that there are physical laws and mathematical principles. It is reasonable to refer to "principles" of learning; however, it should be understood that a principle of learning does not mean that invariably, with all people, under all circumstances, a particular method will give a specific result, or that a specific factor always will produce one particular outcome. Rather, principles of learning should be interpreted to mean general tendencies for learning to take place more effectively under one condition or set of conditions than another.

3   As an example, we will discuss later in this chapter the principle of distributed practice. This means that there is a tendency for study distributed over several intervals to give a greater degree of retention of material than a single period of study gives. This does *not* mean that study broken into several short intervals of time will invariably give all people greater returns of learning than the same amount of study concentrated in one "sitting" would.

4   In other words, the principles of learning express tendencies and probabilities, not certainties. You probably will find that in your own case the principles of learning discussed in this chapter operate in the manner described. On the other hand, you may find an occasional instance where the psychological factor commonly making for most efficient learning does not actually result in your most effective learning. These "principles" of learning, then, should be taken as guidelines, not as immutable laws.

[5] Following the R.S.V.P. procedure will almost certainly increase greatly the effectiveness of your study over an unsystematized just-read-it-over-and-then-read-it-over-again method that you may have been using. With an understanding of the theoretical principles on which the system is based, you can improve the effectiveness of your study even more. The person who is familiar with the "whys" of doing something usually can accomplish his work better than another person who knows equally well the technique of accomplishing it but does not understand the reason for his action. In studying this chapter, as other chapters, use the R.S.V.P. system. This will give you practice in the use of the system and will also result in your comprehending and retaining the material of the chapter more thoroughly than you otherwise would. Therefore, if you have not already done so, pause at this time to PREVIEW the remainder of this chapter. Next, STUDY the chapter, and finally VERBALIZE your own conception of each paragraph. By the time you have done this, you will have a good working familiarity with the factors that operate to promote learning and will understand even more fully just how and why the R.S.V.P. system of study produces more effective learning than simply reading and rereading material does.

Readiness

[6] Have you ever noticed that when you begin to study an assignment it often takes a few minutes for you to "warm up" to your work? For a little while at the beginning of your study period your mind is still drifting around on other things—what you did last night, what you will do when you finish your preparation of tomorrow's lessons, even still lingering on the subject you were studying immediately before you began studying this one. You may be described as lacking "readiness" to plunge your mind fully and unreservedly into the subject you are beginning. Expressed differently, your "mind-set" is not toward the subject that you are beginning to study. Obviously, you will study with greater efficiency when your mind is completely devoted to the subject at hand, with extraneous and competing thoughts excluded.

[7] The REVIEW step of the R.S.V.P. procedure serves an important function in this respect. REVIEWING your previous assignment—doing the hard, taxing, penetrating mental work required to recall and state the meaning of a section or a chapter— is a fast, highly effective means of focusing your mind intently on the subject at hand. It gets your thinking channeled along the lines of the subject that you are studying, gets you into an appropriate frame of mind to understand and interpret the less familiar topics that you will shortly be studying. Obviously,

however, you can achieve readiness—the right mind-set—to study the subject much more effectively if you REVIEW with the *conscious intention* of getting your mind focused on the subject you are about to study. This is the value you obtain from knowing not only the technique to use in study but also the psychological factors capitalized on by the technique. You will study more effectively as a result of getting the proper mind-set for your study through REVIEWING, but also you will REVIEW more effectively and learn more from your REVIEW if you recognize that a part of what you are accomplishing is complete concentration on the subject you are about to study and the elimination of all competing thoughts from your mind.

8 How important is this readiness? You can answer this question for yourself by a moment's reflection. Do you recall having sat down to study at some time when you simply did not feel in the mood for it? Your mind was a regular gymnasium of other subjects, doing handsprings and playing ball games so vigorously that your present subject didn't have a chance to get on the court! You recall how little you really learned about the subject while your mind was one-third or two-thirds diverted in other directions instead of on the subject at hand. You recall how frustrating it was to try to grasp complex material while your mind was still partly lingering on other subjects.

9 The factor of readiness or mind-set is the psychological condition of being prepared, mentally and emotionally, to concentrate on the subject at hand instead of on other things. There is a simple mechanical policy you can follow to increase your readiness and achieve the proper mind-set for a subject more easily. If you will set aside a particular place that you use for study and for nothing else, it will soon become second nature to you to turn your mind toward study when you put yourself in that physical location. A desk containing nothing except the bare essentials of books, paper, pencils, and other necessities that you use in your preparation of assignments, facing a wall where there are no pictures, no reminders, no windows through which the beauties of nature, human or nonhuman, can be observed—such a situation makes it easier for you to quickly focus your full attention on the subject at hand and "get in the swing" of your work. You gradually develop a habit of study when you sit down at the desk, so that in time you find that when you sit down there you can very quickly, almost automatically, exclude all thoughts from your mind except the study you are to perform. You will form the *habit* of concentrating when you sit at this desk, and the habit lowers the amount of effort that you have to expend to get yourself in the mood for studying.

10 Having a regular time to do your studying is another mechanical device that will aid you in quickly achieving good mind-

A Regular Time and Place for Study Helps You Concentrate

set for study. If immediately following a certain class, a certain meal, a certain activity of some sort, you go to your desk and spend the next period of time studying, it soon becomes second nature for other things to fade from your mind at that time in that location. Thus you have your full mental energy to devote to your study, rather than having to expend an important part of it in forcing yourself to concentrate.

11 Combining the psychological technique of REVIEW and the mechanical technique of having a regular time and place for study can enable you to save valuable effort and minutes that you would otherwise have to spend in "warming up" to your study. It can enable you to concentrate with full mental effectiveness almost from the first moment you open your book.

Motivation

12 The stronger your desire to learn, the faster you will learn and the better you will remember what you learn. The stronger your intention to learn, the faster you will learn and the better you will retain what you are learning. The stronger your interest in learning the material you are studying, the faster you will learn it and the better you will retain what you learn. If you have a real desire to learn, an intention to learn, and an interest in learning, you are said to be *motivated*, and the degree of motivation greatly influences how well you learn.

¹³ Of these three components of motivation—desire, intention, and interest—only one can be created simply by an act of will on your part. By sheer will power you can give yourself an intention to learn. How important is the mere intention to learn? You can check this quite easily for yourself. Think back in your memory to the times when you have been introduced to people, have heard their names, and perhaps have even repeated their names after hearing them, but with no intention of remembering those names. Remember how quickly and completely you forgot the names? Next time you are introduced to a person, think of the person's name, say the name over to yourself, and make a firm mental note to remember it. Concentrate hard on the name, with the intention of making it a permanent part of your memory store. A few instances of this will suggest to you the effect that simple intent to learn and remember has on learning and on permanence of memory.

¹⁴ Here is an experiment that does not have to wait until you meet someone. You know how often you have picked up the telephone receiver, dialed a number that you had just looked up in the directory, and when the operator unexpectedly asked, "What number did you dial?" you had not the faintest idea what the number was. You had not intended to remember that number. You looked at it only long enough to hold it in your mind while you were dialing, and then let it go away. But now look up a number in your telephone directory—any number at all will do—and look at it carefully, intently, with the intention of remembering it for a few minutes at least. You will find that the simple study of the number with the *intention to remember* will cause you to hold it much more clearly in mind than you usually do.

¹⁵ Now apply this principle to study. As you study a formula, a paragraph of a history text, or a principle or concept in mathematics, look at that formula, paragraph, or concept intently, and deliberately focus on it with the intention of remembering it. Tell yourself consciously that you are going to remember this particular thing. As you read paragraph after paragraph, page after page, look at each significant fact or idea and tell yourself, "Here is something I am going to remember." This mere fact of reading with a highly concentrated intention to remember will increase amazingly the amount of material that you do remember.

¹⁶ The desire to learn and interest in what you are learning cannot, unfortunately, be created by a simple exercise of will power, as can intent to learn. Desire to learn and interest in what is being learned are rather closely related, although by no means identical. They are related closely enough, however, that the devices you can use to produce one will also tend to produce the other in many instances. For example, you can acquire a desire

to learn simply by reminding yourself that you will be tested in oral or written form on the material you are reading, and your score on the test will influence whether you will receive credit for the course or will have to spend many long hours of preparation and classroom attendance next semester going over the same material again. This is not the most commendable basis for a desire to learn something, but it is an ever-present one in the college situation, and a desire stemming from this basis is much better than no desire to learn at all. If you consciously remind yourself that you must learn this material because you will be held accountable for it on a test and will be searching your mind for it to answer questions, you will find your efficiency in learning and remembering the material stepped up considerably.

17   There are bases for desire to learn and remember other than the motivation provided by the necessity of passing tests. The things that you study in college are carefully selected and designed to be of value to you in living a full, happy, and successful life, coping with the problems you meet, and getting the most out of living. As part of the PREVIEW step of the R.S.V.P. procedure of study, think how the material that you are previewing may be pertinent to some life situation in which you might find yourself. If it is a chemical formula, you may find its usefulness in understanding such phenomena as the tarnishing of silver, the shorting out of an automobile battery, the action of soda, vinegar, or some other substance in cleaning a kitchen pan, or simply the significance of different ingredients in toothpaste or a piece of cloth that you buy. The paragraph that you read in your history book gives you an insight into some aspect of what man has done and the results that came from his doing it. An understanding of what man has done in the past, and what happened as a result of what he did, is probably the best basis that man has for determining his wisest course of action in the future.

18   The point is this: Everything you study in your school assignments is included as a part of your college curriculum because it will help you in some aspect of life—in understanding the political implications of news items, in appreciating the merits and shortcomings of something you read, or in coping with a specific situation that requires you to know what to do and how to do it. There is value in the material you are assigned to study as a part of your college work. Many students never appreciate that value. They look on the material as something to be studied only for purposes of passing an examination.

19   After PREVIEWING an assignment, and perhaps again before beginning the STUDY step, pause and ask yourself, "What is the significance of this topic in producing an educated, com-

petent person, more able to cope with the problems of life, and more able to understand the complex events that happen in the world?" There is potential value for you in every assignment you have in college. The only question is: Do you look at it penetratingly enough and discriminatingly enough to recognize its value? If you do so, if you identify the potential personal value of an assignment, you will find that it works miracles in increasing your desire to remember what you study and your interest in it. It is as simple as this: We are interested in things that we can see are important to *us*. We have less interest in things whose importance to us is vague, obscure, and unrecognized.

20   Students uninterested in a part of their college education typically have not recognized the value that the material holds for them in living successfully and satisfactorily. The baseball player coming to bat has no difficulty in being interested in what his coach is telling him about the strengths, weaknesses, and peculiarities of the pitcher he is about to face. He is interested in learning what he is told because he can see the importance of that information to him in what he is about to do. The widow with a thousand dollars to invest, listening to her broker tell her about different stocks, has no difficulty in becoming interested in what he is saying, because she recognizes the importance to her of the information. Unfortunately, the importance of most of the things you study in college lies in the future; it is not as immediate and pressing as in the case of the ballplayer or the investor. But that importance is there. The person who profits most from his college education, generally speaking, is the person who most accurately and completely perceives the way in which the studies he is pursuing will assist him later on. He profits most not only because his interest leads him to study more, but because his interest causes him to look for the import, the implications, of what he is studying, and therefore he gets a deeper and more comprehensive understanding of the real significance of what he is studying.

21   Thus you can see that an important function of the PREVIEW step is to gain an insight into the general nature of the material you are to STUDY. This will enable you to think through the implications of that material and perceive the place it will fill in rounding out your education and making you a competent, well-educated adult, able to cope with the problems of living and able to understand the significance of things that otherwise would be meaningless or confusing. As you perceive the significance of what you are studying, your interest in both the material itself and in learning it will increase. Your studying will be more pleasant, a more challenging task, and less drudgery. You will study with the aim of understanding the significance and implications of what you are reading, and all of this will result in a

higher degree of comprehension and retention of the topics you study.

Vann planned to major in economics, then try for a job that seemed to offer good opportunity for advancement in some business or industry. As it happened, in his sophomore year he was able to take six elective courses of his own choosing. Vann's interests centered pretty closely around business and commercial areas, but he had selected the following subjects as his electives:

> Shakespeare's Tragedies
> General Sociology
> Abnormal Psychology
> Advanced English Composition
> Political Philosophy
> Survey of the Physical Sciences

When Vann's advisor looked over the proposed schedule, he expressed some surprise at Vann's choices and asked the boy why he had chosen these electives. Vann admitted that he had no especially strong interest in any of them, but he explained the reasons he thought each course might be of value to him in light of his vocational plans. His major advisor was impressed by Vann's foresight and good judgment, as shown by his selection of electives and his reasoning as to their practical value—values that would not have been perceived by most students planning to enter the business world.

How could Vann have justified each of the six electives listed above as being of practical value to a young businessman?

Knowledge of Results

22   You learn better and faster when you are constantly aware of just how effective your study is. When you know the results of your reading, know whether or not you are really getting the material you are going over, you learn more efficiently than when you are going over material without a clear knowledge of how well you are learning it. "Immediate feedback," *i.e.*, letting the student know moment by moment how well he is doing, is one of the chief merits of programmed instruction (often inaccurately referred to as "machine teaching" or "teaching machines").

23   Psychological experiments have revealed that students kept closely informed of how well they were doing in any type of academic performance tended to surpass in performance those students who were not informed of how well they were getting

Knowledge of Results Helps You Improve

along. This is not surprising when you stop to think of it. Knowing how well you are mastering the material you are reading gives you ideas about more effective ways of learning it. If you are learning the material well as you go along, it is likely that you would continue reading just as you have been. On the other hand, if at any time you find that you are not getting the material, you would start looking for the reason for your failure to grasp it. You would check your concentration and try to focus your attention more completely on the subject. You would go a little more slowly, or spend a little more time thinking through the implications of what you have read. You would try harder to relate what you are now learning to your prior knowledge of the field. You would try any of many different devices to change your approach in order to achieve a little more nearly the results you want.

24   Through the years this becomes an unconscious process with a student. By the time you have reached college, you have frequently changed your method of studying a subject without consciously planning to do so. You unconsciously or very dimly perceived that you were not doing very well in learning something you were reading over, and without consciously planning a change of procedure, you altered your method in one way or another. As a result of constantly knowing how well you are learning the material you study, you can from time to time consciously and purposefully change your reading-thinking tech-

nique to eliminate weaknesses, to capitalize on techniques that are proving effective, and to raise your study effectiveness to the highest possible level.

25 This is an important contribution of the VERBALIZE step of the R.S.V.P. method. When, at the end of a paragraph or an assignment, you pause to state in your own words what you have read, you are testing yourself to see how well your method of learning that paragraph or assignment has succeeded. Immediately—not tomorrow, or when the examination comes along—you have a very accurate evaluation of just how effective your study was. If you can state in your own words, without hesitation and without confusion, just what you have read in a paragraph, you have strong evidence that your learning of that paragraph has been effective, and by continuing to read and think just as you have been, you should continue to learn effectively. If, on the other hand, you find that your memory is faulty, or you encounter confusion and fogginess when you try to express what you have read, you realize at once that you have not thoroughly comprehended the material you have read and that something must be done to improve your comprehension before going on to the next paragraph. So, you once more go over the paragraph that you did not master thoroughly in your first reading. This time you probably read it a little bit differently. You are concentrating harder, you are thinking about it in a little different light, and probably when you have read it this time you will be able to VERBALIZE quite adequately the contents of the paragraph. Therefore, as you proceed to your next paragraph, you use the same approach that you used in your successful study of the preceding paragraph, and, as a result, more than likely you learn it thoroughly on your first reading.

26 In the preceding chapter we discussed the value of the VERBALIZING step in fixing material in your mind, but here you should also recognize its value in showing you whether you should continue reading and thinking through subsequent paragraphs just as you did the last one, or whether some changes in your technique are in order.

Distributed Practice

27 Do you learn more and better from studying a subject a few minutes at a time, or by lumping all your study of a subject into one concentrated marathon period of study?

28 The answer to this question cannot be given dogmatically and unequivocally. There are too many variables involved. We must clarify what is meant by "a few minutes at a time" or a "marathon period of study." Some psychologists think a few minutes at a time means study periods of five to ten minutes each.

Others feel that a few minutes at a time means half an hour to an hour of uninterrupted study. Also, what is meant by "distributed"? Is it distributed study when you study for fifty minutes, then take a one-hour break, and then come back and study again? Or, is it distributed study only when you wait until the following day or the following week for your next study period on this subject? Psychologists have obtained highly contradictory results on the question of distributed versus concentrated study periods, largely due to their differing definitions of massed study and distributed practice.

29   Still another factor that has influenced results on this subject is the degree or type of learning you are working for. Concentrated or massed study may work better when you are attempting to get the general idea of a topic you are studying, but may work less well when you are trying to achieve practically rote memory of the material—or perhaps the other way around. Distributed practice might work better on subject matter that is to be studied only for general understanding and less well where rote memory is required.

30   Despite all these considerations and the conflicting results obtained by psychologists (at least partly because of these considerations), the following generalization seems to be justified: Studying material on three or four days, with the total amount of study time being, for instance, two hours, seems to give better results in initial learning and in permanent memory than studying the material in a single study period for two hours and then not referring to it again. This is one important principle of learning that underlies the entire R.S.V.P. procedure. In following the R.S.V.P. procedure you will study a section of subject matter on three successive days. On the first day you briefly PREVIEW it to gain the general idea of what it is about and see how it fits in with the material you have just finished STUDYING intensively. On the second day you go over it again, this time to STUDY intensively and VERBALIZE it. On the third day you REVIEW the material that you have previously PREVIEWED, STUDIED intensively, then VERBALIZED. If, for instance, of a total of sixty minutes spent studying an assignment, you devote five minutes to PREVIEWING, forty minutes to STUDYING and VERBALIZING, and fifteen minutes to REVIEWING, the chances are very great that you will learn it more thoroughly and remember it longer and better than if you studied it for sixty minutes at one sitting and did no PREVIEW or REVIEW of it.

31   Immediately after you finish studying a subject, you begin to forget the material quite rapidly. You forget very rapidly the things that were so fresh in your mind as you VERBALIZED the assignment. However, if you go over that same subject matter again, the rate of forgetting after the second coverage is much

slower and tends to level off at a higher percentage of memory than did the rate of forgetting when you had only covered it once. When the material is covered three times—PREVIEWED, STUDIED and VERBALIZED, and REVIEWED—the rate of forgetting is slow and tends to level off, leaving you with a high percentage of memory of the subject. This is the principle of distributed practice, the principle that material covered on subsequent days, or even with the lapse of a few days between coverages, tends to be retained better than that covered only once, even though the one coverage consumed exactly as much time as was spent in several distributed coverages.

32   The R.S.V.P. method was deliberately designed to take advantage of this principle of learning. The value of distributed practice is one of the important reasons why each step of the R.S.V.P. procedure should be performed in its entirety and on the time schedule described in Chapter Two. Performing it exactly as outlined there actually gives you a higher rate of retention per minute spent in studying than you are likely to achieve any other way.

Meaningfulness of Material

Paul is discouraged. He was slightly above average in his high school graduating class, but he fears he is going to fail both trigonometry and history of civilization this first semester in college. He is puzzled and somewhat defeated because he is studying considerably harder than he ever did in high school and when he finishes studying his daily assignments, he feels that he has learned them well. But the questions his professors ask, both when calling on him in class and on tests, baffle him. They do not ask him to state a rule, or to give a fact—Paul is prepared to do both. Rather, they ask him to do something that, as far as he can remember, was never covered in either the textbook or the classroom. Instead of being given a neat equation to solve, Paul finds himself confronted with a problem about the angles of the sides of a dam. There was nothing like this in the textbook! Instead of being asked to outline the climactic struggle between Athens and Sparta, which he was fully prepared to do from his study of the text, Paul was asked on a test today to compare the role of some leader in that struggle with the role of any historical or contemporary leader in America!

Paul doggedly studies longer and longer. He more nearly commits his textbooks to memory. But he feels himself slipping further and further behind in these courses.

1. How would you diagnose Paul's difficulty?

2. What would you advise him to do to avoid failure in his courses?

3. As you study the following section, identify suggestions for studying that would be most likely to help Paul.

4. After studying the section, look over Paul's case again. Would you now diagnose his difficulty differently, or change or alter your advice to him? Does your earlier evaluation of his problem still seem adequate? Why or why not?

³³ Psychological experiments have indicated—and your own experience and common sense will verify this if you reflect a moment—that the more meaningful material is to you, the easier it is for you to learn and remember. Thus, it is easier for you to learn a list of words in your own language than it is to learn a list of foreign words whose meanings or whose sounds are unfamiliar to you. It is easier to learn and remember a group of words composing a coherent sentence than a group of numbers having only an arbitrary, meaningless association with each other. It is easier to learn and remember a group of sentences that, taken together, tell a story than it is to learn and remember an equal number of sentences of the same length that have no relationship to each other in thought. In short, the more meaningful material is to you, the better you can learn and remember it. This is one of the principles suggesting the use of the PREVIEW step in the R.S.V.P. system of study.

³⁴ By PREVIEWING material that you subsequently will study in more detail, you get the overall picture of the general subject. It was mentioned earlier that previewing a jigsaw puzzle enables you to work with greater speed and effectiveness in putting the puzzle together. PREVIEWING a section or chapter that you are about to study gives you the big picture, the general idea or theme of the topic, and enables you to study each sentence or portion of the topic as one more piece building toward the overall concept that the topic carries, rather than trying to learn each in isolation, as facts or ideas unrelated to other things that you know.

³⁵ Let us look a little more closely at what is meant by "meaningfulness" of material. Suppose that I read a corporate report, a financial report of a corporation. If I have no knowledge of accounting, economics, or finance, the corporate report is not meaningful to me. I do not understand its significance. I do not know the relationship of one part of the report to another part. I do not know how to evaluate, interpret, or relate the information given. The report is, therefore, meaningless to me, and I will probably remember little or none of it. If, on the other hand, I have knowledge of accounting, finance, economics, and management, I can read the report and comprehend its significance.

Because of my specialized knowledge, what would otherwise be meaningless becomes meaningful material.

36 Similarly, in studying any subject—botany, physics, literature, history, or psychology—as you read a sentence or a paragraph you should form a concept of the implications of the facts or thoughts given in light of what you already know of the subject. Suppose, for example, that in a history text you found the sentence, "By the beginning of the twentieth century, it was clear that continued large-scale immigration of populations from other continents to the United States would produce severe problems in the assimilation of these populations into the American culture and into the labor market." One way of treating the sentence is to read the words over, let your brain record them, and pass on to the next sentence. This may give you memory of the sentence, and this memory may enable you at a later time to appreciate the significance of the sentence if you are called on to do so as part of the discussion in class or part of a test. On the other hand, it may not.

37 Another way of treating this sentence is to thoughtfully consider its meaning, significance, and implications. There is the clear implication that immigration to the United States had been large in the nineteenth century. There is the implication that immigrant people tended to preserve their own cultures, minimizing the homogeneity of our nation and making the United States, in effect, more a conglomeration of peoples maintaining separate identities than one unified nation, one culture, and one people. There is the further implication that immigrants posed a special problem in the area of labor. Perhaps they provided more workers than there were jobs. Perhaps they provided competition for jobs, which aroused resentment on the part of native-born Americans or immigrants of earlier years. Perhaps they would work at lower wages, thus constituting a threat to the economic advancement of the native labor force. Which of these labor problems was significant, or were any or all of them significant? This sentence does not reveal the answer, but it alerts the thoughtful reader to the need for supplemental information to round out the implications of the concept that the sentence presented. This is a good example of studying for meanings, implications, and significance rather than merely studying for facts.

38 You may feel that time does not permit you to spend on each sentence in every assignment the amount of time in reflection just illustrated, particularly if you have three to five assignments running from four to twenty pages of reading material each. And you are quite right. However, it will not ordinarily be necessary to spend that amount of time, especially after you develop a little facility in reading for meaning. For one thing,

not all sentences are as packed with implications as the one selected for purposes of illustration here. Following such a sentence the author may have included several sentences that develop the ideas we have presented here as results of your own thinking. In other words, a pithy sentence laden with implications and significance is very commonly followed, sometimes even preceded, by several sentences that provide much of the significance and many of the implications of the key sentence.

[39] Furthermore, the ability to analyze meaty sentences, like most complex mental abilities, develops through practice. You can achieve a high degree of effectiveness, with increase in speed as well as in accuracy of your interpretations, by consciously and systematically working to extract the meaning from what you read. One part of your mind can race through facts, ideas, and concepts that you already possess, shuffling them around and placing the current thought among them to orient it and see how it fits into the big picture, while another part of your mind is actually in the process of taking in the idea more perfectly. If this sounds complex and difficult, let us go back to our analogy of the jigsaw puzzle. You are quite aware that while your eyes and a part of your mind are searching the pile of unplaced pieces of the puzzle, another part of your mind is mentally constructing the possible shape and color and figure content that would go in the hole you are trying to fill. Simultaneously analyzing a sentence, determining the significance and implications of the thought contained in it, and mentally fitting it into your present storehouse of knowledge and concepts of the general subject, is only a more abstract form of simultaneous mental exercise that is represented in working the jigsaw puzzle.

[40] Returning to the financial statement illustration (paragraph 35), suppose you encounter a statement by a stock market analyst who has studied a corporate report. He says, "The price/earnings ratio of this stock is currently 18." If you know something of stocks, the stock market, and the terms and mechanisms used in computing relationships in stocks, you almost instantly, practically without conscious effort on your part, say to yourself, "Well, that means that if the stock earned $1.25 this year, its price is roughly $23.00. If today's market shows it below 23, the price/earnings ratio has gone down. If it is above 23, it is a little more expensive in terms of its earnings. Eighteen is a high ratio for some kinds of stock, but isn't at all high for certain other stocks. Therefore, I have to find the nature, past-earnings record, and, if possible, the future prospects of this company to understand fully the significance of the short sentence quoted." In actual practice, all of this may slip through your mind as fast as you read, and the total process be complete almost by the time you have finished reading the sentence.

41   Similarly, if you practice constantly and systematically studying the sentences you read for their meaning, looking for their implications and significance, you will find that the process will become almost automatic and you can proceed at practically as fast a pace as you have read in the past. The meaningfulness that the material achieves in your mind by this process will add greatly to your retention of it, as well as increase your appreciation of its significance and give you an actual knowledge of the subject you are studying, as contrasted to a mere memory of facts about it. It is hardly necessary to point out that only if you appreciate the significance of the sentence you have read, and grasp the concept that it is designed to transmit, can you apply the concept helpfully in understanding and interpreting new situations or new material related to it.

42   When you have PREVIEWED an assignment effectively, as a part of the R.S.V.P. procedure of study, you are in a good position to STUDY it in a way that will make it most meaningful to you and give you clear and accurate concepts rather than merely a mass of information. In carrying through the VERBALIZE step, you will be testing yourself to see whether you have truly grasped the sense of what you read. Since you will seldom, if ever, be able to recall verbatim the paragraph you are trying to VERBALIZE, you must restate its sense, its meaning. Thus, this system contains a built-in check to see if you are grasping the fundamental thoughts of textual material rather than merely accumulating irrelevant and undigested bits of information. Study thoughtfully. Look for the meaning, the implications, and the significance of what you read. Think about it. Ask yourself, "How does this tie in with the entire subject I am studying? How does it fit in with what I already know? What does it suggest for the future?" Practice will enable you to do this about as fast as you have been accustomed to reading in the past, but studying in this manner will immeasurably increase both your retention of what you study and your ability to use it effectively in discussing topics in class, answering test questions, and in your future professional career.

43   Turn back to the case of Paul (pages 35 and 36) again. Having studied this section on the importance of getting the meaning of what you study, would you change or elaborate on your opinion and recommendations?

Reading Versus Recitation

44   In the discussion of the R.S.V.P. method it was pointed out that psychological experimentation has indicated that reading and then verbalizing what has been read is superior to reading and rereading as a means of learning and retention. There are

How Much Time Should You Spend Verbalizing?

several reasons for logically expecting this result from carefully controlled experimentation.

45   First, reading done for the purpose of immediately restating what is read is more purposeful than reading done with only the vague intent to understand and remember. The intention of putting into your own words what you have read intensifies attention and interest. It gives immediate goals. It raises your motivation to learn.

46   In addition to giving immediate purpose, and therefore greater motivation to learn, VERBALIZING gives practice in analysis and synthesis of data studied. It causes you to react actively and thoughtfully to what you read rather than to simply "go over" the material; the mental exercise of expressing this substance in your own words adds to your understanding of it and fixes it firmly in your memory.

47   Furthermore, thinking through something you read to the point of being able to express the author's ideas in your own words requires thinking and reasoning about the content. To state another person's ideas in words other than his without distorting the ideas calls for thinking through what he said to the point of clear comprehension of it. This is the kind of analysis of thought-content that is necessary in order to be able to apply that material in useful and appropriate places. An understanding going beyond mere rote memory to a comprehension of the sense, the meaning, the significance of facts and ideas is

necessary before those facts and ideas can be applied discriminatingly and appropriately to help you understand or cope with a situation in the future.

⁴⁸ Perhaps a good summary of this whole idea is that before you can VERBALIZE material you have read, you must gain "insight" into that material. You must grasp its essential message. You have to achieve in your own mind the concept it is attempting to develop. From this discussion you can see that the VERBALIZE step in the R.S.V.P. procedure of study is an essential one. You should note that it serves two very different and perhaps equally important functions. First, it increases memory of what is studied, and second, it leads to increased understanding and therefore increased ability to use and apply the learned material.

⁴⁹ How much time should be spent on reading and how much on recitation will vary, of course, from person to person, as already has been indicated. You will have to decide for yourself what proportion works best for you. However, as a rule of thumb, you may safely accept the fact that unless you are sorely lacking in reading skill, your learning will be most effective if you spend a minimum of half of your study time on the VERBALIZING step, and limit your reading to not more than one-half your entire study time. Naturally, this principle cannot apply to assignments involving reading and reporting on a dozen books during a quarter or semester. It is applicable to textbooks and to reference material that needs to be learned and remembered as thoroughly as possible.

Ruth is a freshman at Community Junior College and lives at home. She and her mother have developed a decided difference of opinion. Ruth wants to have a friend come over to her home from time to time so that they can study together. While Ruth's mother does not object to her having friends visit her, she maintains that they get no studying done—they just talk. Ruth admits that sometimes they do spend some time in social conversation, but says that most of their talking is about the assignment they are studying.

Since Ruth is still living at home, her mother regards it as her responsibility to see that Ruth does her studying "properly." And while she does not deny that the girls may spend a large portion of their time together talking about their history lesson, she says Ruth ought to be "studying" her assignments, not "talking about" them.

1. Evaluate Ruth's studying with a friend.
   (a) What are the advantages of two or three people studying together?
   (b) What are the disadvantages?

2. How well does studying with someone work in your own case? Why?

After PREVIEWING this chapter, write your summary paragraph here. Identify the scope of the chapter or the topics it covers.

A DYNAMIC APPROACH TO LISTENING Chapter Four

¹ If only your ears are at work when you are "listening" to a lecture, you will learn practically nothing. Unless your mind is actively concentrating on what is being said, reacting to it, thinking about it, mulling it over, interpreting it, relating it to the things you already know, and filtering out the significance of facts and ideas as they are given to you, the time you spend in a lecture is largely wasted. On the other hand, probably the biggest time-saver in the whole area of studying is effectively listening to lectures and class discussions. So, to get started properly, sit where you can hear the speaker. If you are assigned a seat where you cannot hear the teacher, tell him so. He will allow you to change your seat. Don't be bashful about making such a request. Your professors want you to listen to what they say, and to hear it clearly. The typical professor will bring out in his lectures virtually everything in the course that he believes to be really important. The student who hears, understands, and remembers what the teacher says is almost sure to do well on tests.

² This does not mean that effective listening in the classroom can take the place of outside study, for several reasons. First, prior study of a subject is necessary for most effective listening to a lecture on the subject. Second, you may be asked to discuss a topic or answer a question based on your study of the textbook assignment for the day. Third, study of the text is necessary to fix in your mind details that round out classroom discussion as led by the instructor. But as a college student you are going to spend a certain number of hours in the classroom during a course, and spending those hours most effectively can save you many hours of out-of-the-classroom work!

³ The dynamics of effective learning brought into play by use of the R.S.V.P. system of study are as important in learning through listening to a lecture as they are in learning through reading a book. But it takes more ingenuity and resourcefulness to apply the R.S.V.P. procedure to listening to a lecture than to reading a book. This is but another way of saying that it is harder to learn thoroughly through listening to a lecture than it is to learn through reading a book. This is true. It is more difficult, and for a rather obvious reason. A book is there before you. You can look at it for a while, think a while, skip some material, go back to look again at what you have already read, PREVIEW a chapter, and generally accommodate the intake of material to

A Dynamic Approach to Listening | 43

your own preference and convenience. You cannot do this when you are listening to a lecture. The words of a professor hang in the air only fractions of a second before they are gone forever. You cannot conveniently punch a button and cause the instructor to stop while you mull over what he is saying, while you think through a confusing point, or while you resolve some conflict or confusion in your mind. These conditions render it more difficult both to learn from a lecture and to apply the R.S.V.P. procedure to listening to a lecture. These same conditions, nevertheless, increase proportionately your need for highly effective listening and increase the returns you will get from learning to listen, using the R.S.V.P. procedure.

Previewing a Lecture

⁴ As in studying a book, you can listen to a lecture most successfully and with greater comprehension if you have PRE-VIEWED what the lecturer will talk about. Certainly, this is not as easy to do as it is to PREVIEW a chapter in a textbook. At first glance you may say it is impossible to preview what somebody is going to say sometime in the future. But use your brain, your imagination, your creative thinking ability! From the study assignment you have been given, you usually can deduce with fair accuracy what your professor will talk about in his next lecture. He will ordinarily talk along one of two lines, or a combination of them, and your thoughtful study of the assignment will prepare you to obtain maximum benefit from either course he follows. He may (1) discuss the topics in the assignment itself, elaborating on what is said in the text. In this case, your knowledge of what the text presents enables you to follow his lecture intelligently and with comprehension. He may (2) discuss topics *related* to the assignment but not covered in the text. Your clear comprehension of the textual material will enable you to perceive how the material he is presenting relates to the subject as a whole, and will give you a framework within which to organize and interpret his facts and ideas.

⁵ If, in your normal preparation of the reading assignment, you identify major topics—as you certainly should do in performing the VERBALIZE step of R.S.V.P.—you will have in mind the major topics that his lecture probably will revolve around. Of course, some professors are said to lecture period after period with no perceptible reference to the topic assigned for study. This may be true in an occasional instance. Certainly, however, most professors talk about the topics covered in the reading assignments they have given, along one or both of the two lines mentioned above. A clear identification of what those main topics are and a familiarity with the content of the topics, such as

you will achieve by using the R.S.V.P. method of study, should give you a clear and comprehensive framework of what the instructor will be talking about and the general aspects of the subject he will comment on. This is true for almost all the lectures you will attend in college.

6 Try to sit down in the classroom a few minutes before a lecture begins. Instead of talking to your neighbor, spend those few minutes in looking over the assignment and jotting down on a sheet of paper your idea of the general topics the instructor will talk about during the period. A half-dozen practice periods such as this, each time modifying your prediction on the basis of how well you spotted the pattern of his comments in the last period, will in most cases enable you to prepare a fairly accurate outline of the forthcoming lecture. You will find that three minutes spent in this manner will produce an amazing increase in the clarity of your perception and comprehension of the lecture. (And, generally speaking, your social life is not going to be affected materially one way or the other by these three minutes!)

7 This PREVIEWING, allied to listening, activates several of the factors that promote learning, which were discussed in Chapter Three. It increases your readiness to learn from the lecture, exactly as it increased your readiness to learn from reading, by giving you an overall picture of what you will hear and getting your mind attuned to the subject. It also may enhance your desire to learn because (again, as in the case of PREVIEWING before reading) it gives you a broad conception of the overall pattern and import of what you are about to hear, and thus makes your listening more purposeful and the material more meaningful to you.

8 Finally, note this: You cannot stand in the hall smoking, talking to your buddy or your girl, drop the cigarette and snatch up your books when you hear the class bell ringing, dash in the door just as the bell stops ringing, and flop down into your seat still dreaming of her light brown hair—or planning your strategy—and instantly begin to listen effectively to what the professor says. Those three minutes give you the necessary "getting in the mood" time that you need to get into any new topic, idea, or activity.

Studying a Lecture

9 When the R.S.V.P. method is applied to a lecture, the STUDY step is the process of listening, rather than reading. You should recognize that effective listening is a relatively high-level skill. Some of the procedures described here to improve the effectiveness of your listening are not simple things that you can do automatically. It will require practice on your part to develop skill in doing them, but faithful practice in following these guidelines in

listening to a lecture will enable you to listen with a higher degree of effectiveness and get more from the lecture than you previously thought possible.

¹⁰ The first and foremost thing to remember is that effective listening is an active mental process of *thinking* about what you are hearing. It involves the mental reaction of reasoning, weighing, and analyzing what is being said, not merely opening your ears so the words can reach your mind. Sitting comfortably at your ease, putting yourself into a receptive frame of mind, and letting your brain receive the lecturer's words as they flow into it do not constitute effective listening. You have to concentrate, think, and reason. But do you have trouble making yourself concentrate? Does your mind insist on wandering away from the lecture? Here are some suggestions to help you concentrate, listen effectively to lectures, and learn most from the hours you spend in the classroom.

Look at the Lecturer

¹¹ Do not expect your mind to stay on the lecture when your eyes are wandering to the window, your doodling, or the pretty girl two rows over. It won't. It will follow your eyes. Keeping your eyes fixed on the lecturer does not guarantee that your mind will stay fixed on what he is saying, but letting them stray practically guarantees that your mind will concern itself with something—anything—besides the lecture. (Of course, it is also common courtesy to at least appear to give attention to a speaker!) One exception to the rule of looking at the lecturer concerns note-taking: Obviously, you cannot take notes effectively without looking at the paper. Most speakers feel that note-taking is the most sincere form of flattery and are delighted to observe members of their class or audience busily recording their words and ideas.

Look for the General Plan, the Theme, of the Lecture

¹² As an analogy, consider that the professor is building a house in this course. It is helpful for you to see the sketch of what the whole thing is to look like when it is finished. He has the blueprint, but you have a similar one in the contents of your text. So you have before you the possibility of seeing what the whole course is supposed to be when it is finished. But in every lecture, the professor is building on some specific part of this structure, just as you are doing when you are reading your text. Everything you are studying is contributing to the completion of a total structure; it is also contributing to the building of some specific part right now, so every day you need to see both what you are

currently working on and its relation to the entire structure. Otherwise, if you just start adding this to that, without knowing what you are building, you are much less likely to end up with a complete, well-integrated knowledge of a subject. In building the structure of the course, the professor nails down the points, one by one (sometimes almost literally by pounding out the important things as he tells them). In a preliminary course, you may well only wind up with a sketchy skeleton of the structure when you have finished. As you progress in the field, you make this structure more and more complete and have more and more details and finished work on it.

13 So, to do best in a course, familiarize yourself with the overall structure the lecturer is striving to build. Getting the organization, the theme, or the pattern of each lecture will give you a better understanding of the lecture as a whole and of the course as a whole. It will also help you tremendously in recalling the individual details that went into the construction of this big picture, if you are asked to do so on tests or in recitations.

*Listen for Ideas, Implications, and Significance,
Not Merely Words and Facts*

14 As the lecturer talks, constantly ask yourself, "What is he getting at? What does all this mean? What is the implication of

Fit the Facts and Ideas into an Organized Picture

what he is saying? How does this fit together? What does it add up to?"

15 Your experience in reading paragraphs for meaning and implications, as described in Chapter Two, will prove highly valuable practice in enabling you to listen with analytical discrimination. As you learn to cut quickly and incisively to the meaning and significance of a paragraph you read, you will also find that you can listen to a lecture with much greater perception of the real meaning and implications of what you hear than you could in the past. Naturally, it is necessary for you to learn and remember a large number of facts in your studying and listening, but good scholarship and the desire for knowledge require that you go far beyond mere memory of facts. They demand that you sift and rearrange those facts in your mind to form a meaningful concept of the subject. You cannot do all this without the intense mental activity that is a prerequisite for effective listening— mental activity that involves analysis, synthesis, and interpretation of the lecturer's words. Engaging in it energetically and consistently will do much to ensure that you learn more from the lectures, make better grades on the examinations, and acquire greater knowledge of the field.

Listen for Special Emphases

16 Lecturers use a variety of signals to indicate when they are saying something they consider unusually important. One will raise or lower his voice. Another will say, "The thing to remember is . . ." or other words that show the importance of the point. One may repeat, perhaps in slightly different words, the major points and ideas. Some will pause or speak more slowly when covering a point of unusual importance. Whenever a lecturer enumerates points in "one, two, three" fashion, you can be reasonably sure that they are important points. Since there are so many different ways of indicating the importance of points, no pat formula for recognizing them can be given. Identifying them is up to your own alertness and perceptiveness, but you may be sure that in most instances the cues to important points will be present if you are alert to identify them.

Take Notes

17 Taking a good set of notes on a lecture is the surest single way of concentrating on the lecture and fixing in your mind the ideas the lecturer covers. As a bonus, good notes provide you with a remarkably simple and most profitable means of reviewing what was said. In applying the R.S.V.P. system to listening to a lecture, taking notes becomes the VERBALIZING step, which we will now discuss in more detail.

Make Good Notes   **Bad Ones Are Useless**

Verbalizing a Lecture

18 In discussing the R.S.V.P. system as applied to studying a book, VERBALIZING was said to involve stating in your own words what the author had written. It was pointed out, however, that you actually were VERBALIZING in another step of the R.S.V.P. procedure too. When you were STUDYING and writing brief summaries of paragraphs, or key points, in the margins of the pages, you were VERBALIZING. You were, in effect, making an informational outline of the high spots of what you were reading.

19 The VERBALIZING step in listening to a lecture is taking notes, and taking notes is to the lecture what your marginal notes were to the text. Your lecture notes are literally records of the high points and the most significant details of what the professor is saying. The skill that you developed in making concise marginal notes of what you read will transfer almost totally to skill in making similar notes on a lecture you are listening to, and vice versa. The biggest difference is that in taking notes on a lecture you have little time to think and consider what you are going to write. You must take your notes so fast that your condensation of what you are hearing into a few words must become almost automatic. You do not have time to stop and figure out how to best express what the instructor was saying, or where this particular note should fit into the big scheme of the note-taking pattern that you are using. You must take your notes on the run.

Even this skill can be practiced quite effectively in your reading by forcing yourself to construct your marginal notes briefly and at a high rate of speed, even though circumstances would permit you to proceed in a leisurely manner, thinking them out and carefully inscribing them as slowly as you wish.

20 There are several well-defined principles to learn and follow in order to take notes effectively. Practice and perfect your skill in taking lecture notes by following the guidelines discussed below.

Record the Speaker's Ideas in Your Own Words

21 The necessity of listening for thoughts and ideas in addition to facts and words has already been stressed. When you make a note of a fact or idea the lecturer brings out, put it in your own words. If you can say what he said, but in your own words, you probably understand the topic and are not merely parroting words or phrases. Rephrasing the lecturer's words requires a high degree of mental activity and concentration, which in itself helps you learn and remember the maximum amount from the lecture. Naturally, having PREVIEWED his lecture by your advance study of the subject is extremely helpful here. Without already having in mind at least a sketchy idea of the whole topic, you will hardly be able to keep up with what he is saying and simultaneously translate it into your own words. There are, of course, times when it is best to record the exact words of the instructor. Your judgment is your only resource for identifying the exceptional instance when a verbatim quotation rather than a summary statement is needed for your notes. The practice you have obtained in taking notes on your reading assignments, as described in Chapter Two, will help you quickly build up skill and accuracy in taking good notes on lectures.

Be Brief

22 Do not include such unnecessary words as *a, an,* or *the,* or prepositions and conjunctions that do not affect meaning or thought. Pick crucial nouns, verbs, and modifiers and record these as your notes. Look at the magazine advertisements of "shorthand" consisting of abrvns of wrds wch u cn rcgnz ezly & wrk up ur on s-hnd for not-takg if you wish. (Just watch that this does not ruin your regular spelling!) Using a few symbols for commonly used, hard-to-write words can speed up your note-taking tremendously. But be sure that you write *legibly.* Do not scribble so hurriedly that later you cannot even read your own notes.

23 Above all, do not try to write down *everything* the lecturer

says. This gets back to the first rule—boil down, condense, pick the concentrated grains of thought from his words and write these in your notes. Leave out the embroidery. You are not to transcribe what he says, but to translate his ideas into your own words. If you try to put down everything the lecturer says, you will quickly become disgusted with note-taking and abandon it as hopeless. But if you take notes discriminatingly, you can end each class period with a real addition to your knowledge of the subject. You will find that most speakers space their important ideas throughout their lectures, elaborating with less important, explanatory material in between. This gives you time to get down the important points without falling behind.

Make Notes of Ideas, Not Merely of Topic Headings

24 Do not mistake recording the title of a topic for noting the gist of the topic. Of course, you will not make this mistake if you conscientiously work at recording the speaker's thoughts instead of his words. Your three-minute pre-period outline may well consist of such topic headings, but they are not adequate for classroom notes. A lecturer may be discussing types of legislatures and identify the bicameral and unicameral, with the nature and advantages and disadvantages of each. Be sure that you do not leave the classroom with your notes consisting of the headings he talked about, "Bicameral—nature—advantages—disadvantages — Unicameral — nature — advantages — disadvantages," but omitting what he said under those headings.

Take As Many Notes As You Conveniently Can

25 Of course, you do not want to spend every minute of a class period writing so furiously that at the end of the course you do not know what the instructor looks like, but for most effective note-taking you should count on keeping your pencil fairly busy during a period. Some students fail in their note-taking because they wait for an earth-shattering pronouncement from the instructor before writing anything down on their paper. Most knowledge of most subjects comes in the form of gradual accumulation of significant material rather than in the form of learning an occasional fact or idea of overwhelming importance. By all means, keep your notes brief, but take notes of many things!

26 The correlation between the number of notes students take in class (intelligently designed notes, that is) and their grades on the course may never have been computed, but it probably would be so high as to astound everyone—except the instructors. They know the value of notes! So take notes steadily, even

though at the moment you may not see how this material is very important. When you complete the notes for the period, usually you will see how important ideas emerged from the lecture, even though they may not have been clearly identified as such at the time. And you may be surprised at how closely you find you are listening to lectures in the process of getting these notes!

Systematize Your Notes As Soon As Possible

27 It is probably best to have a loose-leaf notebook with a separate section of notes for each of your courses. This makes it easy to keep all notes on a subject together and to add pages at appropriate places if for some reason you want to elaborate on a topic previously covered. Do not fill every line of your notepaper with as many words as you possibly can squeeze on it. Spread out your notes as you take them. Leave sufficient space so that, as you REVIEW the notes that evening while they are fresh in your mind, you can jot down additional ideas or clarifying words, which you remember but did not have time to get down during the class period.

28 Do your best to indicate major points as you take your notes, by indenting, underlining, numbering and lettering, or any other system that you prefer. As you REVIEW your notes that evening, check to see if your hurried outline form was accurate and satisfactory. If it broke down somewhere along the line, re-number or otherwise change your designations to convert your faulty outline into an accurate one. Also check at this point to be sure that your writing is legible enough that you will be able to read it later.

29 You now see that taking notes on a lecture is actually a form of recitation, or verbalizing, in that you are expressing the ideas of someone else in your own words rather than merely listening to those ideas. Taking notes serves much the same pur-pose in listening that VERBALIZING serves when you are reading a textbook. You will recall our emphasis on how much more ef-fective this verbalization was than merely rereading the pages. In applying the R.S.V.P. procedure to listening to a lecture, verbalization is accomplished in two steps: first, *taking* the notes, which we have just considered, and second, *reviewing* the notes after class, which we will discuss now.

Reviewing a Lecture

30 Just as reviewing printed pages that you have studied is important in fixing the material in your memory, so reviewing your notes on a lecture within twenty-four hours after taking them will aid you greatly in increasing your comprehension and

memory of the thoughts presented in the lecture. We have already mentioned the importance of systematizing your notes. A good time to systematize, perfect, and review notes of the last lecture you heard is when you sit down to study your next assignment of the subject. Reviewing and systematizing notes, fortunately, can be done as one operation.

31   Run through your entire mass of notes on a lecture to see if the organization you used when taking them is adequate. What are the main points? How do the various details fit under these main points? With this general plan in mind, look at the first major point included in your day's notes and designate it by the Roman numeral *I* (if you did not do so when writing it down originally). What subpoints relate directly to it? Indicate each of these subpoints by an Arabic numeral, *1, 2, 3*, and so on. Probably you will have some details that support these subpoints. Some people like to identify each detail by still a further subdivision, the small letters *a*, *b*, *c*, for instance. This you may or may not do, as you wish. Generally, identifying major points and the subpoints directly supporting them is enough to give your outline the system and structure that you need to organize the entire lecture into a meaningful pattern. Additional details usually can be left more or less as you jotted them down under the subpoints.

32   Some students find it desirable to completely rewrite each set of class notes, achieving a beautiful degree of organization and clear indication of major, minor, and subpoints in the rewriting. This is excellent if you have the time. Most students, however, find that they can spend their time more profitably in thinking through the deeper significance of the notes they made than in the purely mechanical process of rewriting the notes. (In fact, rewriting notes as a part of the process of reviewing them can actually *interfere* with good reviewing, focusing the student's attention on the mere mechanics of outlining rather than on proper review.) Your own experimentation will reveal for you whether it works better to take a different-colored pencil or pen, for instance, and insert Roman and Arabic numerals to indicate major and minor points, or whether it pays you to spend the time to rewrite the entire mass of notes, achieving a perfect organization and outline as you do so.

33   Whichever plan you follow, bear in mind that the value of REVIEWING these notes does not lie primarily in routinely reading them over. The real value is in thinking about the significance of each phrase, recalling the elaborations that the instructor made but which you did not have time to write down, and, where necessary, inserting such elaborations as you feel are necessary for a full, permanent record of the real thought of the instructor.

The Payoff at Exam Time

³⁴ This thoughtful REVIEW activates at least four of the psychological principles related to learning. First, it provides you with a knowledge of the results of your note-taking. As you attempt to re-create from your notes the lecture that you heard, you can readily evaluate how adequate or inadequate your notes are, where they need improvement, and where you were unusually successful in capturing the exact thoughts of the professor. Each experience of this type increases your future ability to represent accurately the thoughts of the professor and to avoid omissions or unsatisfactory expressions of what you hear in the lecture. Second, REVIEW also provides you with the benefit of distributed practice. Last night you PREVIEWED the material on which you expected the lecture to be based. This morning you heard (STUDIED) the lecture and took notes on it (VERBALIZED). Tonight, or perhaps tomorrow, you will REVIEW the notes with the double purpose of improving their expression and form and recreating the lecture in your own mind from the information contained in your notes. This gives the material of the lecture another "going over" in your mind. Third, the VERBALIZING you do as you REVIEW capitalizes on the advantages found in recitation as a part of the learning process.

³⁵ Fourth and finally, REVIEWING your notes gives you an unparalleled opportunity to enhance the meaningfulness of the lecture material. While the lecture was in progress, you did not

have time to reflect and draw inferences, interpret and determine the significance, and thoroughly organize and assimilate all of the ideas and facts that were being presented by the instructor. Race your mind as fast as you can and you still find the instructor outstrips you if you pause to think through all the implications of what he is saying. In REVIEWING your notes, however, you are not under this pressure of time. You can determine the significance of the notes you have made and the inferences that follow from things the instructor said. You can study the entire pattern of your notes to clarify your concepts of the overall import and significance of the lecture.

36 All four of these important adjuncts to learning can be achieved to a much higher degree from REVIEWING your lecture notes than from trying to accomplish them while the lecture is actually in progress.

Sam makes it a point to be in his seat by the time the bell rings to begin a class period. As the instructor checks the roll, Sam leafs through his notebook until he finds a clean page, gets out his pencil, and is prepared to take notes whenever something about the instructor's discussion of any topic suggests to him that this is an especially important point. Sam is careful to write legibly and to record exactly what the instructor says regarding anything that seems to be important enough to justify making a note.

Suzanne, Sam's girl, sits across the aisle from him in one class. They do not engage in conversation or write notes to each other during the period, but it is pleasant, Sam feels, to sit where he can see her—especially when the period becomes dull!

Some of Sam's classes consist largely of discussion by students and of questions asked of specific students by the instructor. He studies the textbook assignments for these classes before coming to class. In other courses, the instructors lecture all or most of the time. Sam feels that here he can profitably postpone his assigned reading until the weekend, because he thinks he would have more difficulty concentrating on the lectures if he had already studied substantially the same ideas in the text.

Sam has found that a good many college professors talk a lot without saying anything really important. Their lectures seem to consist of many descriptions, comparisons, and related concepts, with only an occasional really important fact being stated or point made. He concentrates on catching these infrequent noteworthy points and getting them down verbatim in his notebook. He does not bother taking notes about the general and expository material that comes in such quantity between important facts. Sometimes he finishes a period with a full page of notes, and sometimes with none at all.

Sometime during the class period Sam notes at the top of the page the date of the class so that when it is time to review for a test he can identify the notes he needs. When reviewing for a test, he both studies his classroom notes and reads all assigned reading.

1. What suggestions could you give Sam that might enable him to learn more from the classes he attends?

2. What specific suggestions could you give him that would improve the usefulness of his notes? How could he use his notes, once taken, more effectively?

After PREVIEWING this chapter, write your summary paragraph here.

IMPROVING YOUR READING EFFICIENCY

1   How would you like to read half again as fast as you have read in the past—or perhaps twice as fast—with greater comprehension of what you read? Silly question—of course you would like it! Not only would it help you prepare your reading assignments faster, it would also allow you to read some of the other things you would like to read but do not have time for now— magazines, newspapers, and books. Reading half again or twice as fast, without decreasing the amount you learn and remember from your reading, would help you with every college course you take.

2   Twenty hours of proper practice can probably increase your speed of reading by 50 to 100 per cent, and simultaneously improve the degree of your comprehension. Reading-improvement laboratories operated by many colleges and universities and reputable private reading-improvement courses turn out thousands of people who have increased their reading speed by these percentages every year. Many people more than double their speed of reading, and few taking such a course improve less than 50 per cent.

3   Any conscientious student can confidently expect to raise his rate of reading in a twenty-hour course in a reading laboratory. The average American has been accustomed to reading between 100 and 300 words per minute. When he leaves the reading course, he should be reading from 300 to 600 words per minute, and understanding just as much of what he reads.

4   Think of the advantage the rapid reader has over others who take twice as long to read, with no greater comprehension. Think of the time you personally would save if you could do all of the reading you now do in one-half or two-thirds the time it takes you, and comprehend what you read even better than you now do. More time for thinking would be yours, more time for recreation, leisure, or getting other work done. The interesting thing is that you can achieve this 50 to 100 per cent improvement in your speed of reading by your own efforts, without the assistance of any reading-improvement laboratory, by 40 thirty-minute periods of practice of a few simple procedures. Furthermore, you can do most of this practice on your regularly assigned

course reading, and after the first hour of practice accomplish both your study and your reading practice in less time than you had previously spent on study alone.

5 At a meeting of the American Association for the Advancement of Science, an experiment was reported that substantiates this assertion. Two groups of men, of managerial or executive level, were given a 22-hour course in reading improvement. One group took a finely designed, expensive reading-laboratory course, using all the machines such laboratories employ to speed up reading rate and improve eye movement. The other group's reading course consisted of the plan that will be outlined in this chapter. At the beginning of the experiment, the seventy-two men in the "machine-taught" group were reading an average of 217.12 words per minute, and at the end they averaged 315.29 words, for a gain of 98.17 words per minute, or about 45 per cent. The forty-three comprising the "aid-less" group started out with an average rate of 220.23 words per minute and finished at the average rate of 368.29 words per minute, a gain of 148.06 words per minute, or over 67 per cent.

6 Certainly, you would have to analyze more data than these to be justified in saying that people actually improve their reading more by practicing without machines than with them. At the very least, however, the experiment indicated that you need not resign yourself to being a slow reader just because you cannot conveniently go to a reading-improvement laboratory.

7 If you want to read faster and yet understand and remember what you read as well as or even better than you have in the past, study the plan that follows. Get a watch, a pencil, and paper, and start reading faster right now! Here is the reason you can increase your rate of reading immediately, merely by trying to do so: You seldom read as rapidly as you *can* read, just as you seldom walk as rapidly as you can walk. A little practice can develop in your eyes and mind the habit of reading at a much faster pace than you have been in the habit of doing, so that, as you become accustomed to it, you will read rapidly without feeling rushed or strained.

8 This will take more energy and effort than you have been accustomed to spend in reading, but it will save time. Wouldn't you rather work harder on your lessons for four hours, for instance, and get them done well than dillydally on them for six or even eight hours, and then wind up with them done less well? Following the steps to more efficient reading given below and using the R.S.V.P. plan of study will enable you to better prepare lessons that require reading and to do so in less time than you formerly spent partially preparing them. Use this procedure to speed up your reading as a part of your study-improvement program.

Steps to More Efficient Reading

Sit Erect and Hold Your Book Squarely Before Your Eyes

9   Sitting up straight on a hard chair and holding your book upright on a table before you will help you to increase your speed of reading. Having your body alert and your muscles vigorously awake, holding you in a good, healthful posture, makes it easier for you to keep your mind alert, active, concentrating on getting the sense of every line your eyes sweep over.

Practice Reading As Fast As You Can Drive Your Eyes
and Mind to Take in the Material

10   You may use the reading involved in the STUDY step of the R.S.V.P. procedure of study as the greater part of your exercises for practicing speed reading. Drive your eyes to take in the words as fast as they possibly can, and drive your brain to assimilate the ideas fed it just as fast. Your eyes do not move steadily across a line of reading matter. They progress in a series of fixations and jumps. They pause to look at a group of a few letters or words, jump to the next group and pause again, and so on. Fast reading requires that your eyes take in several words at a time and do this in a quick, short pause. Therefore, you should deliberately at-

S–T–R–E–T–C–H Your Eye Span .   Don't See Just a Word at a Time

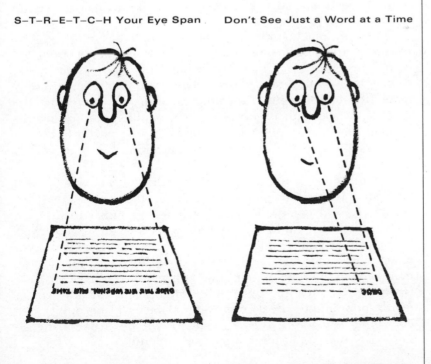

tempt to "stretch" your eyes to take in as long a group of words as you possibly can, and alert your eyes and mind to recognize that group of words as quickly as possible. Keep it up. Never let your eyes drift lazily along the page. Keep them stretching to take in big gulps, moving like a track man running the hurdles, not like a Sunday afternoon stroller meandering along the boulevard! Keep your brain working as hard as your eyes. As fast as your eyes flash the words to your brain, pounce on them with your mind to identify and follow the thoughts the words are developing.

11 This procedure need not interfere with making marginal notes as you read, as was recommended in the R.S.V.P. procedure. Read a paragraph at top speed, then pause to distill its ideas into a marginal note. Go on to read the next paragraph at top speed, then pause again to formulate and jot down your notes, and so on. This high-speed reading of a paragraph, interrupted at the end to make notes of what you read, may impress you at first as unnatural and jerky. If you think about it, however, you will see that it is quite logical. You are learning not merely to read novels faster but to *study* faster, to mentally ingest and digest ideas with maximum speed and efficiency. This requires swift reading accompanied by and appropriately interspersed with reflective thought, not just marathon speed reading. If you will exercise the same effort to formulate and write your notes swiftly that you do to read rapidly, you will learn to take notes at high speed too. This skill, of course, will greatly assist you in taking class notes on lectures.

12 As you practice reading efficiently rather than lazily, your eyes will gradually come to take in larger and larger groups of words, faster and faster, and do it with less and less conscious direction of your brain. This leaves your brain increasingly more free to concentrate on understanding and digesting the flood of facts and ideas your eyes are providing. Performing this mental digestion requires that your brain exert itself to the utmost to keep up with the meaning and significance of the words your eyes take in.

13 Built into the R.S.V.P. plan is a method of checking to see if your brain is "reading" as fast as your eyes. If you can VERBALIZE accurately and comprehensively when you finish reading an assignment, your brain has done its work as well as your eyes. If you cannot VERBALIZE what you have just read, let your eyes move a little more slowly on the next reading, and leave a little more of your energy for your brain to expend. You have not truly improved your reading by merely running your eyes over more words per minute. Real improvement takes place only when *your mind is working at a higher degree of effectiveness*, digesting what you read faster and more completely.

Keep a Record of Your Reading Speed
for a Thirty-Minute Daily Practice Period

14 To develop maximum reading speed, it is helpful to run daily speed checks on your reading rate. Occasionally reading your advance assignment in the PREVIEW step instead of scanning it can provide material for your speed checks, and your REVIEW step may occasionally take the form of rereading, as a speed exercise, the material you have previously PREVIEWED, STUDIED, and VERBALIZED. You may use reference reading or assigned parallel reading for your practice period. You may use your recreational reading, or newspaper or magazine articles, or books, but whatever you select, arrange to spend about thirty minutes each day in an unbroken session of reading as fast as you can make your eyes pick up the words and your brain comprehend them.

15 As part of this rapid-reading exercise, you should compute the average number of words you read per minute in each of your practice sessions. Do you remember the discussion in Chapter Three about how knowledge of results of performance tends to increase subsequent performance? This principle holds true to an exceptional degree in developing your reading speed. If you keep a record of the average number of words you read per minute on a speed trial each day, you have an accurate representation of just how much progress you are making, and can compete with yourself to improve from period to period. Numerous studies have indicated that keeping an accurate record of words read per minute is a most important part of improving your speed of reading, because it warns you if you begin to ease off and lapse into old habits of lazy reading.

16 On the following page there is a form that will assist you in computing your speed of reading and keeping a record of your progress. Keep a record of each of your speed-reading practice sessions for forty days. By reading down the last column, you can follow clearly the increase in speed you are achieving in your reading. To use this form, count the number of words on a typical page or column of the publication you are using in your speed-reading practice. Record that number in the column headed "Words per page." Write down the exact time that you begin your speed practice session, and note the time you finish. Record the number of pages (or columns) you have read in the third column, titled "Number of pages." Multiply the number of words per page by the number of pages you read to get the total number of words read, and record the result in the fourth column. Record the number of minutes you spent reading in the fifth column, headed "Reading time in minutes." You may wish to use an alarm clock and time your reading for an exact

Daily Record of Practice Exercises in Speed Reading

Day	Words per × page	Number of = pages	Total number of ÷ words read	Reading time in = minutes	Average words per minute
1					
2					
3					
4					
5					
6					
7					
8					
9					
10					
11					
12					
13					
14					
15					
16					
17					
18					
19					
20					
21					
22					
23					
24					
25					
26					
27					
28					
29					
30					
31					
32					
33					
34					
35					
36					
37					
38					
39					
40					

thirty minutes each time, and in this case you will always record the number "30" in this column. However, your thirty-minute speed-reading session may be broken up between three or four different articles or short topics that you are reading. In such a case, you would want to record the information for the formula on each of these bits of material separately.

17 In the last column you see the heading, "Average words per minute." This figure is obtained by dividing the total number of words you read by the reading time expressed in minutes. Of course, on some days the material that you read will be more difficult than other material and will require that you read it more slowly. However, over a period of several weeks you should find that the general trend of your average words read per minute is upward—that is, as time goes by, you are tending to read faster and faster.

Check Your Comprehension by Verbalizing All That You Read in Your Speed Exercises

18 An earlier warning is worth re-emphasizing here: Reading *faster* is not reading *better* unless your improvement in comprehension equals or exceeds your increase in rate of reading. This fact requires that you keep constant check to ensure that your speed of reading is not outrunning your speed of comprehension. While you are reading, your mind must be working as hard and as efficiently as your eyes to accept, organize, and make a part of its store of knowledge the material that you are reading. Some so-called "reading-improvement laboratories" neglect this important factor of checking the comprehension of their clients. As a result, they sometimes report utterly fantastic rates of reading— as high as 3,000, 4,000, and even 10,000 words per minute!

19 Well-designed reading-improvement courses, such as those conducted by the various colleges and universities and reputable reading-improvement laboratories, do not claim such reading rates. Even granting the dubious possibility of the human eye being physiologically able to focus on and perceive several thousand words per minute, it is most improbable that the mind could assimilate information at that rate.

20 We repeat: One does *not* improve his reading by merely training his eyes to move over a page faster; real improvement occurs only when the mind is assimilating information at a faster rate, and with as much thoroughness, as previously. VERBALIZING provides a check on this crucial point—are you *learning*, not merely *looking*, faster? Fortunately, experience has shown that the ability of the mind to assimilate material swiftly and accurately is also improved by energetic, purposeful practice. Thus, the increase in reading speed achieved through intelligent efforts

to take in material with one's eyes at a faster rate usually can be paralleled by proportionately increased ability of the mind to assimilate that material swiftly, if the reader is as conscientious about comprehending what he reads as he is in striving to increase the number of words he can see in a minute.

[21] If you work to increase your speed of perceiving words, and in the process of doing so, conscientiously gear your maximum speed of coverage to what your mind can take in as you go, almost certainly you will find that you can increase your speed of reading from 50 to 100 per cent, with no decrease in the amount you recall from your reading. In fact, it is a widespread finding of reputable reading laboratories that increased speed of reading more often than not is accompanied by a slight increase in comprehension of the material read. In other words, the person who increases his speed of reading from 300 words per minute to 600 words per minute, striving meanwhile to train his mind to take in all that his eyes cover, finds that he is actually remembering more of every page he reads at the rate of 600 words per minute than he was remembering at the rate of 300 words per minute. This may seem strange to you, but it really is not. The mind, as well as the eyes, has simply become accustomed to operating at a higher degree of efficiency than in the past. But constant check on comprehension of what is read is essential to prevent the sacrifice of reading improvement for mere increased reading speed.

[22] For best results in improving both the quality and rate of your reading, it is imperative that you practice driving your eyes and your mind at their maximum capability *most* or *all of the time* you are reading. Actually, you will improve conspicuously in your reading speed and comprehension simply by performing the thirty-minute practice exercises each day and nothing else, but your improvement will be much more rapid and, more important, your preparation of schoolwork will be more effective if you will practice speed reading all the time you are reading.

Valerie would be pleased if her reading efficiency were improved, but she is not sure it would be worthwhile to try. After all, she has been reading now for twelve years or so and probably has spent several thousand hours reading. She sat down and calculated, in fact, that in high school alone she must have spent about three thousand hours reading, for this would represent only three hours of reading a day. As far as she can perceive, she reads little if any faster now as a college freshman than she did when she was in the the tenth grade.

It stands to reason, Valerie says, that if you are already reading as fast as your mind takes in new facts and ideas, reading faster will necessarily mean that you get less of what you read.

Valerie already concentrates quite well on what she is reading, so she could not increase her comprehension just by paying closer attention to what she is reading. Keeping a record of how fast you read, Valerie reasons, would be a mere waste of time—when you have read something, recording how long it took does not help you read any faster! And how on earth, she asks, could only twenty hours of systematic practice in increasing reading effectiveness really make any difference?

1. How could a few hours of practice in speed reading improve Valerie's speed of reading when she has been reading for thousands of hours?

2. If Valerie already is fully concentrating on what she reads at her current speed of reading, how could she read faster and still comprehend as much of what she reads?

3. What are the benefits of keeping a written record of your speed of reading when you are trying to learn to read faster?

Scanning

23   Effective performance of the PREVIEW step, described in Chapter Two, requires the ability to scan written material effectively. Scanning consists in running your eyes down a page, not trying to look at every word but merely reading enough here and there to get the drift or trend of the material. You probably will find that the most effective way for you to scan is to run your eyes down the middle of the page in a zigzag pattern, trying to stretch your eye span to pick up a few words from the sides of the page from time to time. While your eyes are doing this, your mind should be hunting hard for the main theme or thought the author seems to be driving at in the paragraphs you scan. Note particularly the first sentence in each paragraph, and also give a longer glance at the last sentence of a paragraph. Writers are more likely to put general indicators of what they are discussing in these sentences than in the ones in between.

24   When scanning an assignment to PREVIEW it as a part of the R.S.V.P. procedure of study, be sure that you do not omit writing the short summary paragraph at the end. If you cannot produce such a paragraph, you did not scan well enough. Try again—scanning takes, after all, only fifteen seconds or so per page, and you can afford to repeat it. Tomorrow, when you STUDY thoroughly the assignment you scanned today, check this summary at the end. If it still seems to summarize pretty accurately what the author said, you did a good job of scanning!

25   In reference or supplemental reading, where your purpose is to acquire a broader acquaintance with a general subject area, and most particularly where you are looking for some specific information in your reference reading and have to cover a large

number of pages to find it, scanning is a lifesaver. With the skill you can acquire within 20 three-minute practice periods of scanning, you can save numerous hours of tedious, unnecessary, and often unprofitable reading. If you are a slow reader, scanning may be the *only* thing that will enable you to complete all the nonintensive reading expected of you in college. Naturally, if you read slowly, you are likely to scan more slowly than faster readers will; but even so, scanning can speed your coverage of material tremendously. While "covering" material is not a satisfactory substitute for "learning" it, intelligent "coverage" is a lot better than neglecting the reading entirely!

26   The key to efficient scanning is fine coordination between the eyes and the mind. The eyes run down, or zigzag down the page, picking up clumps of words here and there. The mind watches those words and works to deduce swiftly and accurately their meaning and implication. It is on the alert to slow down or halt the eyes if it perceives an important point that needs more attention, and it encourages the eyes to move at their maximum pace if the material seems to be relatively routine or of minor significance. The eyes gradually learn a pattern of swinging back and forth down the page, feeding the bits of sentences or paragraphs to the mind as rapidly as possible, so that the mind does not have to give a portion of its attention to the physical business of keeping the eyes moving effectively.

27   Vigorous practice of scanning will prove a great help to you in increasing your rate of detailed reading. The eyes and the mind that learn to work as an effective team in the concentrated work of scanning will read faster and more comprehendingly than eyes and minds that have not acquired the degree of skill and coordination required for good scanning. Any way you look at it, learning to scan is a valuable academic exercise!

After PREVIEWING this chapter, write your summary paragraph here.

¹ Thought is mental digestion. In its most immediate form it involves digesting the food delivered to the mind in the form of information through reading, listening, or any other means by which we gain information. And just as our body can at a later time call upon the energy provided by digested food to accomplish tasks, so can our mind, through another type of thinking, call upon the knowledge we have achieved to help us accomplish mental tasks with which we are later confronted.

² From the foregoing, you may have arrived at the conclusion that there is more than one type of thinking. You are correct. We can distinguish at least four types of thinking. The first, *daydreaming*, letting our imagination have free play without providing direction toward a definite goal, is one type of thinking that all of us engage in from time to time, but one that we will not discuss in this chapter.

³ Another type of thinking is *thinking to understand*. This is perhaps the simplest form of directed, purposeful thinking. It is the form that we use all the time we are studying to convert the words of the author into meaningful mental food, which we then proceed to digest through further thought.

⁴ A third type of thinking is *creative thinking*, in which we attempt to go beyond the limits of previous knowledge or natural combinations of previous knowledge and come up with something absolutely new. James Watt engaged in creative thinking when he conceived the idea of using the steam from a teakettle to run machinery. A boy engages in creative thinking when he conceives a new (to him) way of achieving an acquaintance with a girl whom he wishes to meet.

⁵ A fourth type of thinking is *thinking to solve problems*. This is a highly complex type of thinking requiring skills that distinguish man's mental processes from those of lower animals. It involves both thinking to understand and thinking creatively. In this chapter we will discuss the latter three types of thinking— what they consist of, how they are accomplished, and their place in the life of a college student.

Thinking to Understand

⁶ If your mind registers each word that your eyes pick up from this page, or each word that your ears pick up from a lecture, but registers them only as words, not weaving them together into a larger thought pattern that the author or the lecturer is trying to convey, you are reading or listening without thinking. At this

low level of mental activity you are merely understanding what the various separate words are, but not at all understanding the meanings they convey. For practical purposes, you have wasted even the minute amount of effort you have expended in such an activity.

7 When, however, your mind begins to associate each separate word stimulus into a pattern of stimuli that you recognize as a fact or idea, you are engaging in the first step of mental digestion, which psychologists refer to as converting sensations into perceptions. For practical purposes, you might consider this as converting stimuli (words, sounds) into *information*.

8 If you are studying effectively, you go even further than merely grasping the content of the different sentences the author or the lecturer presents and you perceive the significance and implications of this information. Your mental digestion now is operating at a higher level, and is converting information into *knowledge* by this process. Thinking to understand involves thinking to answer the question, "What does it mean? What are the thoughts the writer or lecturer is trying to convey?" This is truly thinking to learn, thinking to comprehend, thinking to get the meaning—not merely the words—of what you hear or read. It is considerably more strenuous thinking than is involved in merely recognizing the words and getting the faint "drift" of what the lecturer or author is presenting.

9 Thinking to understand may operate at an even higher level of complexity. You may consider this as thinking to *interpret* and *apply* what you read or hear. At this level of thought, you are not only understanding, grasping the full meaning of what an author or lecturer is presenting, but you are swiftly and imaginatively sifting through your previously gained knowledge and correlating what you are now hearing or reading with your previous store of knowledge. You are asking yourself, "How does this fit with what I have learned in the past? How does this change the ideas and concepts that I have held in the past? What are the implications of what I am hearing or reading? What is its significance? How should it affect my way of thinking, my opinions, how I do something?" At its highest level, thinking to understand means not merely thinking to grasp the meaning inherent in sentences, but to interpret the sentences and perceive their significance and implications in terms of the larger body of knowledge of which they are a small part, and to apply that knowledge wherever appropriate.

10 Your interpretive thinking is operating at a relatively high level if, upon reading a newspaper notice that a higher minimum-wage law is being passed, your mind swiftly runs through a process something like this: "That means that some of our lowest-paid workers will be getting more money. This will mean

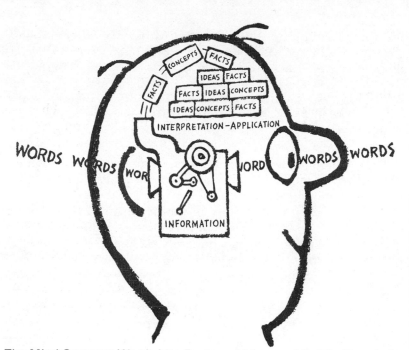

The Mind Converts Words into Facts and Ideas and Builds Knowledge of Subject from Them

that they will have more money to spend in retail trade. That will mean more money in sales tax, and in individual income tax. On the other hand, it is uneconomical to pay more than a certain amount for certain jobs. Some of those jobs may be eliminated if the minimum-wage proposal goes into effect. This will mean greater unemployment and loss of retail trade. It will mean drain on welfare funds and union funds." You are thus grasping not merely the fact you read but also its implications and significance to you and to society.

11   You read Emerson's statement, "Great men have been perceivers of the terrors of life and have manned themselves to face it." At the lowest level of thinking to understand, you merely recollect those words as a sentence. At a somewhat higher level, which we termed "getting the meaning of what you read," you may say, "This means that great men—that is, men who are fine, noble, or outstanding—recognize that there are terrifying and disturbing things in life, but rather than attempt to avoid life's terrors, they brace themselves to face them and live the sort of lives they want to, despite them." At the still higher level of drawing interpretations and inferences and making applications of this concept—thinking to interpret and to apply—you may say, "If I agree with Emerson, I may attempt to increase my stature in

life through training myself to meet life's uncertainties with courage, to accept disappointments and tragedy and still continue to strive to make of my life what I want it to be. In the last analysis, the success or failure of my life will not be determined by circumstances and outside forces but by the courage, resolution, and effort I create within myself as a means of reaching the goals I have in life." This is not to say that this concept or this interpretation is necessarily true of life, but it illustrates the process of penetrating to the genuine significance and implications of what you read or hear, rather than being content with a mere memory of words.

12   The student who studies or who listens to a lecture in this manner is probably deriving the maximum possible value from his college education. He is not merely accumulating an impressive body of facts and knowledge, but he is developing his capacity to use the knowledge that he gains to enrich his own life and influence his perception of the things he encounters in life. People who manage to achieve a college degree without making any appreciable progress in this type of thinking sometimes are referred to as "educated idiots." This is a misnomer, because they are not really educated. They have simply learned, for a longer or shorter period of time, a great many facts. Nevertheless, the expression is a meaningful one, implying as it does that a person completed a great deal of academic work without having learned the secret of making his life and work more effective as a result of the experience he has undergone.

13   If you were to ask a thousand college professors what they would choose if they could change their students in one characteristic and one characteristic only, a high percentage of them would say, "I would have them *think*—think imaginatively, think of the interpretations, the implications, and the significance of what they study." The VERBALIZE step of the R.S.V.P. procedure encourages this thinking, but ideally the thinking should be carried far beyond even converting the author's words into your own. This conversion suggests, however, if accurately accomplished, that you have thought to the extent of gaining the meaning of what you studied. Thinking of interpretations, implications, significance, and applications must depend almost exclusively and inevitably on your own resolution, effort, and resourcefulness.

    Pamela is studying the settlement of Jamestown, Virginia. She has read that it was founded by men without money but of England's upper class, men who thought of the New World as a place where fortunes could be made quickly through finding gold and precious stones. She also learned that they almost starved and were plagued by strife, discord, and quarrels.

1. How would the PREVIEW step help Pam gain a better understanding of the problems of the Jamestown colony?

2. How would the VERBALIZE step ensure that she gets the essential ideas of the assignment?

3. If Pamela thinks to the point of determining the significance and implications of what she has read, what are some of the ideas or concepts she might reach as to the

(a) significance of the type of settlers at Jamestown in relation to the difficulties they had?

(b) type of people who made the best settlers?

(c) reason why the English colonies generally grew to be more permanent than those of the French?

Thinking Creatively

14 Obviously, creative thinking is required for the highest level of thinking to understand. Calculating the effect of a just-learned fact or idea on other aspects of the subject, or applying a fact or idea to one's own activities, is thinking creatively.

15 Similarly, in thinking to solve problems, creative thinking looms large, particularly when it comes to formulating hypotheses. Creative thinking is involved in preparing an assignment such as, "Design an experiment by which you would be able to determine. . . ." Since thinking creatively plays such a large part in the highest levels of thinking, it is well to understand what creative thinking involves, and perhaps how you can cultivate your ability to think creatively.

16 In its purest form, creative thinking may be said to be the thinking that goes beyond the known and beyond the routine use of a known procedure to solve a problem. It is pioneering thinking, thinking "where the mind of man has never set foot"— or, at least, *your* mind! After all, you personally can think creatively about a subject that others already have thoroughly explored if you are not acquainted with their explorations and therefore must depend on your own mental efforts.

17 Creative thinking often involves combining old ideas in a new way. If you are taking French and wish to devise a more effective method of studying it than you have used in the past, you have a good opportunity for creative thinking—using old ideas in a new combination. You have studied French and have learned some French, and therefore know in a general way what you need to learn. You have now studied the R.S.V.P. procedure of learning. Can the R.S.V.P. procedure be applied advantageously to the study of French? Yes, it can. But in this book we

are not going to explain the application of the R.S.V.P. procedure of study to each of your college subjects. You can, however, design your own application of this method to your study of French, or any other foreign language, and through creative thinking you can evolve your own more effective plan of study by a new combination of previously known facts and procedures.

18   You can think creatively by applying knowledge in areas or ways in which such particular knowledge has not been applied before. Creative thinking of this sort might suggest that you use your flair for quick, simple line drawings to illustrate an English composition you are to write. How about using your knowledge of mathematics to determine how great an inaccuracy will be produced in a speedometer and odometer of your automobile if you use a different-size tire than that for which the car was designed? Combine both your knowledge of mathematics and your ability to construct simple charts, graphs, or illustrations to show in an economics term paper the relationship between the portion of the gross national product represented by freight carloadings and the fluctuations of the stock market in a given period. How can the detailed study of note-taking and outlining that you did in English composition be used advantageously in your biology course?

19   All these areas portray creative thinking in various forms. If there is one key to successful creative thinking, it probably is this: Search your mind for facts, ideas, procedures that you can adapt to some subject, topic, or problem in a way that you have never done before. Creative thinking includes such approaches as: (1) how it can be done differently, (2) how something can be applied to it that has never been applied to it before, and (3) how it can be looked at from a different point of view than ever before. By thinking creatively you should be able to add still other paths of creative thinking to these three.

20   One of the most profitable areas of creative thinking for the college student is to look at a class assignment with a view to conceiving questions that logically can be derived from the facts and ideas, but which the author does not formulate. The student who asks numerous intelligent questions that go beyond the bare statements of a textbook or lecture is engaging in an exploratory type of creative thinking. He is thinking, "What if . . . ?" "What would cause . . . ?" "Why is . . . ?" and so on. If he thinks and studies and examines references until he is able to answer the questions he has posed, his creative thinking is going still further, but *asking* intelligent questions on a subject is the starting point of creative thinking. In fact, Thomas A. Edison is reported to have said, "I can find ten men who can find the answer to questions for every man I can find who can conceive a crucial question to be answered."

21   At times creative thinking may be capricious, but always it is based on some foundation of fact and understanding. Otherwise, it is reduced to only random and vapid "wonderings." We all have heard the student who presents an elaborate daydream of an idea, which he obviously thinks is a new approach to a situation—and it *is*, perhaps because it is based on such a completely inaccurate understanding of the basic known facts and principles that no one with the least knowledge and understanding of the subject could possibly come up with an idea like that! This can hardly be called creative thinking, even though the student obviously created the idea all by himself.

22   You see, thinking creatively is not thinking at random any more than scientific experimentation is grabbing various flasks in the chemistry laboratory and pouring some of the contents together at random. In creative thinking and in chemical experimentation, you start with known facts and look for applications, combinations, or procedures that are different from those you are accustomed to, and, from a logical point of view, give promise of producing constructive results or achieving a constructive objective.

Ray has been appointed chairman of the Senior Ball Committee. His high school class of 140 will graduate in June, and he wants to make the ball an unusual event that will long be remembered by all his classmates. He is trying to think of some idea that would constitute the basis for planning a spectacular and impressive event.

Ray could proceed in his thinking in either of two ways. He might dream up an extravaganza that would really be spectacular and surely be long remembered, but that for various reasons would be impossible for his senior class to sponsor. Or he might think equally creatively, but keep within the bounds of reality that must limit the ball.

1. What are some ideas Ray might hit on that would make the ball a long-remembered one, but that probably would be impractical?

2. What are some ideas within the realm of reason that Ray might think of to make the ball what he and his committee want it to be?

3. What criteria must Ray apply to his creative thinking to render it constructive in this situation?

4. How might letting his imagination range unfettered, writing down all ideas he and his committee had, no matter how fanciful or impractical, help Ray finally come up with a practical yet unusual idea?

5. From your thinking on these four questions, state a rule that Ray (or you) could follow to get the maximum help from

free-ranging imagination and still wind up with a practical idea for the ball.

Thinking To Solve Problems

23 Many professors and many textbooks emphasize using knowledge to solve problems quite as much as they emphasize gaining the knowledge itself. A good short definition of the purpose of a college education would be "to enable graduates to more effectively solve the problems of life that they encounter, using both the knowledge of facts and ideas and the skills in thinking, reasoning, and problem solving that they have acquired in college."

24 In a course in economics, the problem may be in the form, "What would be the best way of achieving a . . .?" or "What would probably be the effect of . . .?" In literature it might be, "Which of the stories in the *Canterbury Tales* best reflects a social condition that exists in our own day? Justify your answer." In psychology it might be, "Design an experiment that would indicate the degree to which common superstitions influence the activities of selected college students." Problems in mathematics, chemistry, and physics are too well known to require illustration here.

25 These vastly different types of problems all require certain fundamental procedures for their most valid solutions. The techniques and specific operations involved in the implementation of each step will vary from subject to subject and even from problem to problem within a subject; however, the fields of logic and philosophy have identified certain fundamental steps common to the solution of most types of problems. Let us look at one version of these procedures for problem-solution.

Step 1. Identify the Problem

26 Often this is not as simple and straightforward as one might think. What appears at first glance to be the essence of the difficulty in reaching an answer to a question may, upon more mature consideration and as more knowledge is gained on the subject, prove not to be the real crux of the problem. In a problem in algebra, for instance, finding the "answer" to the problem may be a very simple matter when the verbally stated problem has been restated in the form of an equation. The true problem was the formulation of an equation, not the relatively simple matter of solving the equation once it was formulated.

27 In the illustrative problem based on the *Canterbury Tales*, the true problem may, with study, be found to be not the selection of the tale that is most closely paralleled in our present

society, but the selection and presentation of evidence to substantiate whatever choice is made.

28 In another area of life, many a businessman seeking to increase the volume of his business in order to increase his earnings has found that not his volume but his profit margin was the element that really had to be increased to achieve his desired result.

29 It is frequently impossible to determine precisely the nature of a problem upon your first approach to it. Frequently you must use your best judgment as to what the crux of the problem is and proceed to subsequent steps, always bearing in mind that subsequent developments may require you to re-evaluate the nature of the problem you are trying to solve. What you at first thought was a problem of genetics may instead develop into a problem of how to select the sample to be studied. Conceivably, your history problem of explaining the breakup of the Whig party may prove to be not an analysis of a political party and its tenets as much as an analysis of social change taking place in an era. Spend some time on this step of problem-solution, and do the best you can in the beginning to properly identify your problem, but work toward a solution of it with a conscious alertness to the possibility of having to change your conception of your problem as you go along.

Step 2. Gather Data

30 In geometry, the data to be gathered may be a judicious selection of pertinent axioms, theorems, and possible procedures. A problem in literature may involve collecting the views of various critics and the study of other writings comparable to the one that your problem centers on. It may involve identification of procedures and principles in literary criticism that apply to the specific situation you are dealing with. In history, it may mean marshaling a formidable array of facts regarding the social, economic, political, domestic, and foreign conditions prevailing during the era in which your problem is based. In psychology, it may require gathering both the results of many experiments conducted on subjects similar to the one your problem involves and evaluations of these experiments made by psychologists other than the experimenters.

31 If you are running an experiment, gathering your data may involve designing and conducting an experiment and putting the results of it into usable form. Some problems involve surveys of public opinion or of current conditions in a particular area to provide the data required for solution. Some types of problems may involve extensive laboratory research. A problem in physics will require identifying appropriate principles and procedures

and ways in which these principles and procedures may be applied to the solution of the problem at hand.

[32] As data are gathered, the identity of your problem frequently is seen to change, and you perceive your real problem to be quite different from what you originally thought. As often as this happens, change your conception of your problem to conform to what the weight of evidence indicates it to be, and adjust your research to bear on your re-evaluated problem.

[33] In all except the shortest, simplest problems, where the solution begins to emerge very early, clearly, and with relatively little effort on your part, you will find it necessary to record your data in some form. A loose-leaf notebook with a page devoted to each major area or topic on which you are gathering data may be required in the case of problems in psychology, literature, the social sciences, or similar fields where extensive library research is needed to obtain all the information. If a chemistry, physics, or mathematics problem threatens to be especially difficult for you, you almost certainly will find it helpful to jot down all principles, procedures, concepts, and so on, that you can recall that seem to have a possible bearing on the problem. This may not be necessary in the overwhelming majority of your scientific and mathematical problems, but is an excellent "low-gear" device for keeping clearly before you the full range of resources you have to work with in solving an especially difficult problem.

[34] Selecting methods and combinations of facts and principles, which together may lead to the solution of a problem, is frequently much simpler if all of the facts, principles, and procedures that you must choose from are presented in black and white. By this means you can look at them all at once and concentrate on selecting the proper ones, rather than having to divide your energies between remembering all those you may choose from and simultaneously attempting to evaluate each one and arrive at the proper choices and combinations.

Step 3. Analyze Data

[35] Examine the data and see what the findings add up to, what they mean, what they suggest. Do they suggest that the use of the binomial theorem may solve the problem? Do they suggest that an increase in the weight of a tree comes from its intake of water and air rather than from the soil? Do they suggest that there are areas in which your data are insufficient and that more data must be gathered before the pattern becomes clear?

[36] Many people who have attempted to teach problem-solving as a skill have found that this step is the most difficult one to

teach. This is because most of the steps in problem-solution can be performed at least somewhat "by formula"—that is, by working according to fairly specific and definable rules—whereas analysis of data depends heavily on the professional judgment of the individual. It depends on your ability to look at the data you have gathered and evaluate their significance. Analyzing data, more than any other step, requires that you have studied a subject enough to be competent to evaluate facts and concepts within that subject.

³⁷ In cases of mathematical and scientific problems, properly analyzing data involves studying the various possibilities, procedures, and principles you have gathered and determining which ones are most applicable to the problem at hand. In courses involving primarily reading, data analysis generally involves studying each reference to the problem you have gathered to evaluate its meaning and significance, and then accurately estimating the pattern that the evidence is forming. In this step, too, your concept of the identity of the problem frequently may change, so do not be surprised or dismayed if, in the process of analyzing your data, you find it necessary to restructure your conception of what the problem is. This is not only legitimate but quite common.

Step 4. Formulate Hypotheses

³⁸ By this we mean designing possible courses of action that might lead to the solution of your problem, or, in some instances, making several "educated guesses" as to what the solution might be. An hypothesis is sometimes defined as an assumption made or an idea advanced for the purpose of testing its soundness. That, essentially, is what you do in this step of problem-solving, and the key principle is to formulate as many hypothetical procedures or solutions as you can. Keep your problem in mind, look at your data and your analysis or interpretation of their significance, and say to yourself, "One solution (or procedure) would be to . . . ; another would be to . . . ; then I might go at it this way . . . ; or I might try. . . ." Each of your hypotheses is a possible solution to your problem—either a possible conclusion which might be drawn from your data or a possible procedure by which a solution might be reached.

³⁹ If your problem is one for which one and only one answer is correct, and if you can determine when you have arrived at that answer, you formulate hypotheses until appropriate testing shows that you have found one that gives the proper answer. You might have such a situation when solving a problem in mathematics, for instance.

⁴⁰ In the humanities and social sciences, and in other fields

where there is seldom one clear-cut answer to a problem, you generally will find it best to formulate a number of hypotheses before testing any of them to see which is best. In such areas, as in your everyday life problems, formulating hypotheses in the process of solving problems usually consists of making a list of hypothetical conclusions that might be drawn from the data, or of designing several different hypothetical ways of processing (analyzing and interpreting) your data, hoping that one of the ways will prove good. It would certainly not be acceptable to formulate only one or two possible solutions to such a problem as, for example, how to combat prejudice. Achieving the best possible solution to a problem is most likely when you conceive as many hypothetical solutions as you can. This gives maximum chance of your having thought of the best solution, or of having formulated hypotheses that can be combined to achieve the best possible solution. Your competence in creative thinking makes the vital difference here.

[41] In this phase of problem-solving, do not try to evaluate your hypotheses to determine which are good and which are not good. This will come in the next step. Here you want to construct as many hypothetical solutions or hypothetical procedures by which you might arrive at a solution as you can, because the more you have constructed, the better the likelihood that you will have thought of the best solution to your problem and not just a solution that may get you by.

Step 5. Test Hypotheses

[42] In mathematical and scientific problems, try the procedure you hypothesized might solve your problem, and see if it does indeed solve it. In other areas, use your imagination, your knowledge of the total subject, and your ability in critical thinking to evaluate what the ultimate outcome of following your hypothetical solution would be. To solve the problem of finding ways of combating prejudice, for example, you might take as an hypothesis, "Legal prohibition of discrimination in housing would be helpful." To test the hypothesis, you would try to think through what the most probable results of such legislation would be. You would consider, among other things, the probable public reaction to depriving people of control over the use of their property. You would decide whether this housing measure would be effective in combating discrimination, taking into consideration not only the merits of the plan but also the probable reaction of the people involved.

[43] If analyzing data effectively requires the highest degree of knowledge of the field, testing the hypotheses probably requires the highest degree of perceptive imagination.

44 When you find that following one of your hypotheses to its ultimate conclusion, with all its implications and side effects, leads to an unacceptable result or, as nearly as you can evaluate its probable outcome, would fail to solve your problem, you can do one of three things: abandon that hypothesis, attempt to modify the hypothesis so that its essential weakness would be avoided, or see if it could be combined with another hypothesis in a way that would circumvent the original defect.

45 Test all your hypotheses, even though fairly early in your testing you may identify one that seems quite certain to give a satisfactory solution to the problem. This is because you might not only find an even better solution through another hypothesis, but, more likely, you may find another hypothesis that could be combined with your satisfactory one to give an even more satisfactory solution. Thus, in combating prejudice in housing, a judicious combination of legal action and education through the schools might well promise, on careful evaluation, to give a better result than either would give alone.

Step 6. Draw a Conclusion

46 In many instances, drawing your conclusion proves to be the easiest of the six steps toward problem-solution. Once the

I. My problem...
II. The facts are...
III. These facts mean that...
IV. It might work to either:
    1. zvzvzvzv zvzv
    2. zxzx zxzxzxzxz zx
    3. xvxv xvxvxv xv
    4. xvxvxv xvxvx xvxvxv
V. How would each one work out?
VI. 4 and 1 meet my needs. 3 is a possibility. I'll...

Thinking to Solve Problems

first five have been competently performed, the final one often becomes fairly easy to accomplish. This is not always the case, of course. Sometimes testing the hypotheses reveals *no* solution that you can consider even minimally satisfactory. In such a case, you must determine whether more data, more analysis, more hypotheses, or more testing will provide a better solution, or whether you must achieve the best solution you can from the material you now have to work with.

47 Sometimes the evidence suggests several conclusions with so nearly equal promise that selecting one in preference to another is difficult. Sometimes this can be solved by a combination of procedures that makes possible a conclusion integrating two or more important aspects originally conceived as constituting separate solutions. Sometimes you must weigh the advantages and disadvantages of each solution and accept one that falls far short of what you would like but is the best available or achievable. Actually, as you may have seen by now, drawing a conclusion requires a continuation of the testing step to ensure that the solution selected is in truth the best one available.

48 Most people go through life meeting their problems with guesses, "hunches," and hope. Many manage to achieve rather satisfactory lives by this method. However, there are few people whose accomplishments and lives could not be improved by more frequent and skillful use of thinking to understand, and, more particularly, thinking creatively and solving the problems they face in a deliberate and systematic manner, rather than depending on hope, guesses, and the way they *feel* about the situation.

49 As previously stated, one of the chief purposes of college is to show you how to think more effectively and to encourage you to apply your thinking more extensively and effectively to the problems of your everyday living. Practicing all three types of thinking throughout your college career will not only make you a better educated person but will give you valuable experience in thinking creatively, reasoning, and solving problems, which can help you manage your entire life more effectively.

Sue has a problem. A normal course load this semester would put her within four hours of fulfilling all requirements for junior college graduation—in the middle of the school year. Since she has a low B average, she probably could get permission to register for an overload and take the four extra hours. She has a part-time job in a department store in town, likes it, and plans to work in the store full time when she finishes her college work. She is undecided whether to take the overload and finish in January, or to follow some other course of action.

Using your knowledge of college and of jobs, the procedure of problem-solving you have just studied, and your imagination, draw up an outline showing factors Sue might consider and what additional information she may need to arrive at a well-thought-out solution to her problem in contrast to making a snap judgment. Use the outline below and jot down what Sue might think of and do in each step in reaching her decision.

1. What is the real decision Sue has to make? How might her problem be stated differently from, "Should I take an overload and graduate early?" How many ways could Sue consider her problem?

2. What other facts or information does she need to make a sensible decision?

3. List several different "pictures" that might develop as Sue analyzes her data, depending on what the data turned out to be.

4. List as many hypothetical courses of action as you can think of that Sue might follow.

5. Test each course of action by evaluating its advantages and disadvantages.

6. What criteria would you use, if you were Sue, in deciding which of the different possible courses of action you would finally decide to follow?

After PREVIEWING this chapter, write your summary paragraph here.

EXPRESSING YOURSELF WELL IN CLASS

Chapter Seven

1 Many teachers emphasize daily grades quite heavily in determining course grades. Even a teacher who relies on objective tests throughout a course will be swayed by his memory of a student who, by his intelligent comments and discussion in the classroom, displayed more than a perfunctory interest and knowledge in the field. Classroom participation is especially significant in the numerous instances where the test-score average puts a student right on the borderline between two grades. This means that your final grade may be affected by how well you participate orally in class throughout the course.

2 There are three common classifications (types) of oral activity in which the student may be expected to engage in the classroom: answering questions, contributing to class discussions, and making reports. Each requires preparation before class. Your effectiveness in each of these activities is affected by certain skills having little to do with your knowledge of the subject. Here are some suggestions on how to prepare yourself for oral participation in class activities. Following them will do much to give you a good set of daily grades and allow you to face examinations with the confidence that comes from having a high course average up to that point.

Answering Questions Asked by the Instructor

3 Always remember that the professor is interested in your scholarship, not merely in your memory. This means that he is interested in how skillfully and intelligently you answer questions, as well as in the factual accuracy of your answers. Haven't you heard some student *finally* answer a question correctly, but only after wandering so awkwardly and uncertainly around in the process that you could hardly tell what he was talking about? Haven't you heard an instructor say the equivalent of, "I think you probably know the answer to that question, but I can't be sure from what you are saying!" Obviously, such answers do not deserve or receive as good a grade as answers that are to the point, saying everything that needs to be said and little else. The student who gives a rambling answer may know the facts as well as the one giving a concise yet complete and accurate answer,

Expressing Yourself Well in Class

but it is obvious that he does not have the same clear perception of the topic as the person who can weed out nonessentials and still include the important points.

4 The process of summarizing each paragraph, described as an essential part of the R.S.V.P. procedure of studying, is excellent practice in preparing to answer questions lucidly and accurately. If you follow it up by a check-back in which you try to reconstruct mentally (VERBALIZE) the paragraph from the marginal summary you wrote, you should be able to answer almost any question on the paragraph either briefly or fully, as you find your instructor prefers. For additional security and to polish your technique of orally answering questions to the finest point, practice formulating questions on various paragraphs and answering them aloud. VERBALIZING responses developed to answer specific questions will work wonders in improving the clarity and effectiveness with which you display your knowledge in response to an instructor's question.

5 For best answers, begin to analyze the question and consider the best way of answering it as soon as the professor starts asking the question. By the time he calls your name, you have had a few valuable seconds in which to organize your thoughts.

6 A good practice is to give a brief, accurate answer first, and then elaborate on it, bringing in supplementary details to the extent that you have noticed this particular instructor likes. This is part of the art of answering questions well; some instructors like students' answers to be as comprehensive and detailed as the student can manage, while others prefer short, concise answers covering the bare essentials as succinctly as possible. Throughout life we have to learn to adjust to the differences between the many people we live with and work with and for. It is not unreasonable to expect that you determine the type of answer each of your professors likes and tailor your responses to his preferences.

7 A word of warning: If you do not know the answer to a question asked you directly, it is better to say so. Do not try to bluff or hide your ignorance behind an avalanche of words. The professor can tell whether or not you know the answer, and he will resent your wasting the time of the class attempting to hide your ignorance. You will get a failing grade anyway, and earn his justified irritation by your effort to outsmart him.

8 Some instructors ask for a volunteer to answer questions, either with or without his being specifically recognized. Instructors appreciate a student who can be counted on for worthwhile ideas in response to questions posed to the class at large. Take advantage of such opportunities to demonstrate the quality of your thinking and knowledge; but remember to watch the instructor for cues that indicate he would like you to wait and give

others more opportunity to collect and express their thoughts to a greater extent.

Participating in Classroom Discussions

9 Rather than lecture or ask questions requiring specific answers from certain individuals, some teachers prefer that the class members enter into an exchange of opinions and ideas— that is, a gradual exploration or development of a topic by general student discussion. This is because the teacher knows the value of having a person say in his own words the gist of the matter under consideration. He knows that the average student can gain much by verbalizing. This is where there will be a conspicuous difference in the showing a student makes if, in his lesson preparation, he has tried putting the facts and ideas presented in the text into his own words, in contrast to having merely read the text without VERBALIZING. When such class discussion is initiated by the instructor, you may be sure that he is following the discussion carefully, not only to guide it if necessary but also to note the students whose participation gives evidence of good, average, or poor mastery of the ideas and facts of the subject under discussion. Whether you show up well in a discussion and make a valuable contribution is not a matter of chance but of proper preparation and attitude. Here are some suggestions that may help you.

Prepare for the Discussion

10 You know the subject that will be discussed. It will have been assigned. Read up on it. Think about it. If you can, read three or four references on the topic in addition to your text. And practice VERBALIZING the subject. If you can get together with someone else in the class and talk about the subject the night before, do so. The practice of actually discussing the topic with someone is fine preparation, but just practicing expressing yourself on the subject through the VERBALIZING procedure may help you as much or more.

Ration Your Participation

11 Talking too little and talking too much are equally objectionable. If everyone talked too little, the discussion would die. If all talked too much, there would be chaos instead of orderly discussion. Ideally, of course, everyone should participate approximately equally in a discussion. This is seldom achieved, but it gives you your cue as to how much to participate. If you are naturally reticent, you may need to force yourself to partici-

pate. You have a responsibility to do your part in the discussion. Also, if you have something to say, you had better force yourself to speak up—otherwise, the professor has no way of knowing that you know anything at all about the topic under discussion, and your grade is likely to reflect this. If you are by nature a talkative individual, you may need to check your talking to see that you do not monopolize the floor.

Be Calm and Objective

12   The purpose of most discussions is to stimulate intellectual, not emotional, activity. If your feelings begin to be aroused, drop out of the discussion temporarily, or permanently. You will injure yourself in the eyes of everyone else, as well as lose your own self-respect, if your participation is dominated by your feelings and prejudices rather than by objective evidence.

13   Intellectual honesty requires that you not mix your personal beliefs together with objective facts and present the mixture as all fact. Distinguish between fact and your opinion, where appropriate, when you speak. "It seems to me . . .," "My interpretation is . . .," and other such identification of opinion, used appropriately, will make you a more valuable participant and will impress your fellow students with your reliability and your instructor with your perceptiveness.

Keep Your Contributions Pertinent

14   The purpose of the discussion is to explore a given subject, not to furnish you a ready-made sounding board for your ideas—unless your ideas are appropriate both to the discussion and the participation rights of other discussants. Be careful not to meander off the subject just because you personally are interested in a line of thought that goes off at a tangent. You might be able to give a highly detailed discourse on some special aspect of the subject under consideration that would be somewhat pertinent, but not essential. In such a situation, ask yourself whether the group would be interested in hearing your lengthy contribution, and govern your course of action accordingly. To do otherwise gives evidence of a conspicuous lack of judgment on your part as to the relative importance of various aspects of the topic.

Listen Carefully and Keep Up with the Discussion

15   Have you heard a person speak up in a discussion along some line that simply was not *timely*—make a contribution that was not appropriate to the subject under consideration at the

moment? Being an accurate, perceptive listener is an absolute prerequisite to being a good discussion participant. It is the only way you can avoid repeating what others have said, bringing in untimely or inappropriate topics, or talking too much yourself! Thorough preparation prior to the discussion will stand you in good stead here, for if you have a good knowledge of the whole topic, you will be able to fully concentrate on what others are saying, rather than having to expend most of your thinking trying desperately to remember something out of the textbook. Only by paying attention to what the others are saying can you make your own contributions meaningful, and certainly having a good background of knowledge of the topic is a prerequisite for appropriately judging your own and others' statements and their pertinency. Refrain from starting your own subdiscussions with one or two other participants. This is as rude in a discussion period as during a lecture!

Try to Help the Group Explore the Topic Constructively

16 Do your part to help the leader (or teacher) keep the discussion on the track, keep it moving, keep it off trivia and personalities, and keep it headed toward a general group understanding of the subject being explored. Do this by making your own contributions appropriate and by not being led astray when others lose sight of the goal of the discussion. Be permissive and tolerant of others' contributions. Never resort to ridicule or sarcasm. Try to express disagreement with anyone in words that will show no scorn or disrespect for his ideas, even though they differ from yours.

A psychology class is discussing the relative importance of job security versus opportunity for advancement in a college graduate's choice of a job. Students differ sharply in their opinions, with Vince and Pete finally emerging as the most vocal of the students holding opposing opinions. The following discussion between the two is recorded verbatim:

PETE: The person who doesn't want to advance, to make more money and get a better job, isn't the sort of man a good boss would want on *any* job.

VINCE: There're lots of jobs in the world that have to be done that are at a low level. Jobs that *have* to be done. Somebody has to do them. How would a boss run a place where everybody on those jobs was discontented and unhappy because he wasn't getting promoted? It's ridiculous to say a person isn't fit to be employed as a janitor if he doesn't want to become president of the company! A man may be a fine worker on his particular job, but just not be able to do things that take more brainpower.

PETE: Automation is taking over the sort of jobs you are talking about. Our text told about a study that showed that the lower the level of the worker, the more he was likely to be absent from work and the more he went from one job to another. That's what you get with workers who are not ambitious. They're not responsible. You can't count on them.

VINCE: Just because a fellow's dumb doesn't mean he's a bum! He may be just as good as you would be at the sort of job he can do.

PETE: You're talking about the man who *can't* advance, is not intelligent enough, or something. I'm talking about the person who doesn't *want* to advance, who isn't willing to make the effort or take the chance to get ahead—who is satisfied to just stay in a rut.

VINCE: What about a man's family? They've got to eat. He's got to have money to support them. A job where he can be sure of a regular paycheck beats one with a brilliant future where he may be fired any day, or the job be done away with.

PETE: As his family increases he'll need to make more money. What he's making when he first takes a job may not be enough when he has a bunch of kids and they start to school and all.

VINCE: You don't have to get another job or get promoted to make more money. Nearly all jobs give periodic raises if you stay with them long enough, and the unions are getting wages raised all the time.

PETE: I read a piece in the paper the other day quoting a report from some government agency that unemployment was higher among low-level workers than high level. You aren't as secure in your job at the bottom as you are higher up the ladder.

VINCE: Well, what do you want out of life anyhow? Just a lot of money? Just scrambling around and stomping on people and stabbing them in the back so you can get ahead of them? I'd rather have time to spend with my family and have some free time to go fishing than to work so hard to make more money that I never had a chance to enjoy it.

PETE: I can't argue with you. You won't stay on the subject.

VINCE: Who's arguing? I'm just pointing out some facts to you!

At this point the professor interrupted the discussion.

1. Summarize in a few words the point of view upheld by Pete. By Vince.

2. What have the participants in this interchange actually discussed?

3. Point out faults in the reasoning or participation of Pete. Of Vince.

4. How worthwhile do you consider this discussion to have been? What conclusions do you think Pete and Vince would have agreed on?

5. How do you think Pete would describe the "average low-level worker"? How would this differ from the way you think Vince would describe him? How do these differing underlying feelings show themselves as the discussion progresses?

Making an Oral Report

17 The third common type of oral participation likely to be required of you in class is making an oral report on a book, reference, or experience. There are three distinct elements that determine the quality and effectiveness of an oral report. Listeners may not consciously analyze the talk and realize that it was strong or weak in this aspect or that, but the total impression of a report is determined by a combination of these elements: (1) content, (2) organization, and (3) delivery. Each of these elements must be worked on deliberately and systematically for the report to be good. None of them "comes naturally" to a speaker, nor can weakness in any one be compensated for by strength in the other two—like the wheels of a child's tricycle, all three must be in good shape. There are plenty of books on public speaking in your college library that will give you detailed instructions on how to make an oral report. A few are listed at the end of this chapter. However, if you will observe the following simple guidelines, you usually will give a report that will be of interest and profit to your classmates and reflect credit on you. Here, in brief summary, are the highlights of the recommendations of teachers who specialize in preparing people to speak to an audience.

Content

18 *Determine How Long You Should Talk.* This is an essential preliminary, because until you know your time limits you do not know how broad the scope of your talk can be or how much detail you can include.

19 *Gather Information on the Topic of Your Report.* This usually will be done by library research, and the librarian will assist you in locating the information if you need help. Even if your report is about something you are thoroughly familiar with, finding what others have thought and written on the subject

Research   Organize and Outline   Practice

usually will help you make a clearer and better report. Keep working at this step until you are sure that you have all the raw material you will need for a talk of the length you are to give. Since you may not know exactly what turn your report is going to take, or be able to clearly ascertain the main points until you have all the data together and go over them all, you may need to collect more material than you think you can use. You will be sure of being able to get your message across if you have collected enough material so that you can be selective in what you use.

20   *Decide What Overall Fact, Idea, Principle, or Impression You Wish to Convey.* Do not plan your talk in terms of "covering" a given body of facts or amount of material. Decide what principal message you wish to convey, and select the material necessary to put your message across, not to "cover the subject."

Organization

21   Many coaches of aspiring public speakers say that deficiency in this phase of speech preparation is the most common and the worst fault of trainees. Some say that poor organization of speeches commonly accounts for more loss of potential results than poor content and poor delivery combined!

22   *Select a Few Main Ideas To Get Across.* Choose a few main ideas that carry your principal message, and then spend the necessary time to substantiate them with details and drive

them home. Your audience, including your professor, will have a much higher opinion of your report if it clearly emphasizes a few key ideas that develop your one main theme. Identify these points clearly, and make it clear when you are supporting or discussing one of these main points. Even if you are reporting on the life of some notable person, pick the principal eras, incidents, or characteristics of his life and build your talk around them as main points. Do not merely give a detailed chronology of his existence, but decide on the overall impression you should give of his life, and tailor your points to develop that picture.

23   Restrict the number of your main points to from three to seven. In a ten- or fifteen-minute report, it probably would be unwise to try to include more than five. Too many "main points" cease to be main points at all and become a confusing clutter of details. Pick your truly important ideas or impressions and build them up. Beware of minute detail.

24   *Make an Outline.* Indicate first of all the overall objective, aim, or central theme of your talk. Then list main points, with space to insert subpoints as required. *This is essential!* Only by thus refining your thinking on the content and organization of your talk can you have any assurance that it will "add up" as you want it to. Below is an example of one good outline form for a talk having four main points.

Subject:
Objective of talk:
Introduction:
Body:
    I.
        1.
            a.
            b.
        2.
        3.
            a.
            b.
   II.
        1.
        2.
            a.
            b.
   III.
        1.
        2.
   IV.
Conclusion:

25 *Omit Irrelevant or Unnecessary Material.* Leave out material that is "good stuff" unless it supports one of your main points. If it is important enough to include, decide *why* it is so desirable, and develop it into another major point. Unrelated bits of information cloud the issue and obscure your main theme.

26 *Examine Your Outline Critically.* Carefully examine your outline and the material you plan to include, and decide whether *you* could follow it and would find it interesting if you knew nothing about the subject and were listening to a fellow student give the talk. If your answer is "No," look for ways to improve it.

Delivery

27 *Practice Your Report.* Stand up before a large mirror and deliver your report exactly as you expect to deliver it to the class. If you will stand behind a lectern or a desk in the classroom, rig up a reasonable facsimile for your practice. If you will be speaking in a fairly large room, accustom yourself to looking toward those in the back of the room as well as toward those in the front row.

28 This rehearsing in front of a mirror is important. In no other way can you tell how you will look to the people to whom you are speaking, whether you have awkward mannerisms that will detract from your delivery, whether you look stiff and stilted. Even the best conceived and organized talk loses in effectiveness if it is not delivered well. If it is absolutely impossible for you to find a mirror you can use, go through all the other steps—stand up and rehearse your report aloud, just as you propose to give it. No matter how thoroughly you have thought through what you plan to say, you usually will find that actually saying it produces problems or impressions you recognize as undesirable and will want to change.

29 It is an interesting fact that few professional or semi-professional speakers will consider giving a talk of any kind without repeatedly rehearsing it aloud, timing themselves, while amateur speakers seldom want to rehearse. The importance of practicing your report aloud cannot be overemphasized. You will not give a good report without doing it!

30 *Time Your Report.* In most instances, your estimate of how long it will take to present the material you have decided to include will be a little over or under. If you want to make a good impression with your report, do not talk more than 10 per cent *less* than your allotted time, and do not run overtime *at all*. Critically review your materials and discriminatingly add to or cut out as necessary to tailor your report to the assigned time limits.

31 *Do Not Read Your Report.* Only a master of public speaking or a public figure whose position renders it necessary for him to choose each word deliberately can read a report to an audience without losing much of his potential good effect. Use notes if you wish, but *do not read your report verbatim.* Adults generally do not like to be read to! This is additional reason for your being thoroughly familiar with what you are going to say.

32 *Stand Erectly.* Stand up straight; do not slouch or prop yourself up. Let your hands hang naturally at your sides if you can, clasp them behind you, hold something (your notes?) in them, or gesture with them for emphasis—whatever you like—but do not just tinker with things, especially with things in your pockets. You occasionally may see fine speakers who violate this principle. If you are sure that you are a fine speaker, you may do so, too, but while you are learning, follow the rules.

33 *Speak Clearly and Distinctly, Using Good Grammar and Diction.* Speak loudly enough to be easily heard and understood by those farthest from you. Not speaking loudly enough is one of the commonest faults of the amateur speaker. When speaking in public, it usually is desirable to talk more slowly than your normal rate of speech in informal conversation. This is additional reason for having timed a full-dress rehearsal of your report. Avoid "ummm" and "ahhh," called *vocalized pauses* in the language of public speaking. If you cannot think what to say, glance at your notes, stand silently, and collect your thoughts. This is better than mumbling. Be sure to use correct grammar and diction. Slang has no place in a classroom report.

34 *Stress Your Main Points.* By your voice, by actual statement, or by some other means, let your audience know when you are making a major point. You know how much better you can follow a lecturer who does this. Do it yourself!

35 *Finish Your Report Decisively—Do Not Just Trail Off.* You have heard people get to the end of a very good report (or any other type of speech) and not know how to stop. They twist and squirm and hesitate, ummm and ahhh, and then they may wind up saying rather apologetically, "Uh, uh . . . well . . . I, uh, uh, guess that's about alllll," and slink down into their chair. This sort of anticlimax can ruin the effect of all they have said up to that point. If your talk is to last more than five minutes, you may want to memorize a summary for your finish. Take perhaps a minute to say, "So we see that . . . ," quickly summing up what you have said. End with a note of confident finality in your voice, then sit down! If you do not summarize, rehearse your last sentence carefully so that, with no hesitation, no uncertainty, you can finish your talk with a good strong sentence.

Rita is worried about the report she has to give tomorrow in sociology class on causes of juvenile delinquency. She has a lot of notes on the subject and has studied the guidelines that help to produce a good report, but she is not sure she will be able to follow them properly.

She rides home on a bus with several classmates and decides to ask them what faults or shortcomings they remember having noticed in other students' oral reports. As they think of various ones and tell about them, Rita makes a mental note not to do *that!*

1. Evaluate Rita's procedure thus far in preparing to give the report.

2. What faults or deficiencies do you remember noticing in students' oral reports?

3. What ways can you suggest to guard against each of these errors?

References

Arnold, Carroll C., Douglas Ehninger, and John Gerber. *The Speaker's Resource Book.* Chicago: Scott, Foresman, 1961.

Arntson, Dorothy H. *Beginning College Writing.* Chicago: Scott, Foresman, 1963.

Cromwell, Harvey, and Alan H. Monroe. *Working for More Effective Speech.* Chicago: Scott, Foresman, 1964.

Estrin, Herman A. *Technical and Professional Writing: A Practical Anthology.* New York: Harcourt, Brace & World, 1963.

Godfrey, James W., and Geoffrey Parr. *The Technical Writer: An Aid to the Presentation and Production of Technical Literature.* New York: John Wiley & Sons, 1959.

Hackett, Herbert, *et. al. Understanding and Being Understood.* New York: David McKay, 1957.

Jones, E. Winston. *A Guide to Effective Speech.* New York: David McKay, 1961.

Monroe, Alan H. *Principles and Types of Speech,* 5th ed. Chicago: Scott, Foresman, 1962.

Oliver, Robert T. *The Psychology of Persuasive Speech,* 2nd ed. New York: David McKay, 1957.

Peabody, George E. *How to Speak Effectively,* 2nd ed. New York: John Wiley & Sons, 1942.

Schultz, Howard, and Robert G. Webster. *Technical Report Writing: A Manual and Source Book.* New York: David McKay, 1962.

Sears, Donald A. *Harbrace Guide to the Library and the Research Paper,* 2nd ed. New York: Harcourt, Brace & World, 1960.

Souther, James W. *Technical Report Writing.* New York: John Wiley & Sons, 1957.

Sypherd, W. O., A. M. Fountain, and V. E. Gibbons. *Manual of Technical Writing.* Chicago: Scott, Foresman, 1957.

After PREVIEWING this chapter, write your summary paragraph here.

PREPARING
A WRITTEN
EXERCISE Chapter Eight

¹   A general text on the dynamics of effective study does not afford space to treat fully the various considerations falling within the scope of preparing written reports. Only the broadest, most fundamental guidelines can be presented here. Any good textbook on English composition will provide more detailed guidance on the various topics outlined here. Several references dealing with various aspects of report writing in more detail are listed at the end of this chapter.

²   Most written exercises that college students are required to perform (disregarding completion exercises and highly structured writing, such as laboratory reports) fall into two categories: (1) reports written primarily for the content involved, and (2) reports written primarily to develop skill in composition and rhetoric. These two objectives are by no means mutually exclusive. An instructor who requires a term paper in a history course or a research paper in psychology is both interested in and impressed by the literary quality of the product he receives. He resents misspellings, incomplete sentences, and poor composition. The English teacher who assigns a composition is also interested in its thought content. The most beautifully written composition that contains only trivia and inanities is not a good composition, even though its prose is smoothly worded and its punctuation perfect.

³   Having recognized clearly that both composition and content are important in all reports, we should also acknowledge that the *relative emphasis* varies with the specific situation. In a report on an historical, psychological, or philosophical subject, the greater relative emphasis is on the content, whereas in a composition written for a course in basic English or English composition, the primary emphasis is on composition, including grammar and rhetoric, although in advanced composition courses thought content and composition may be accorded the same importance.

⁴   The first and perhaps most neglected principle in preparing a good written paper is: Start Early! Preparing a good paper takes time. It seldom is done racing a deadline. Professors generally will agree that procrastination, allowing insufficient time for the job, is the biggest single cause of poor written work. If you seriously want to prepare a good paper, plan your time so that you will be able to complete it well *before* the date on which it is due.

Steps in Preparing a Paper

⁵ To produce a creditable paper, you need to attack the task of writing it in a systematic way. Although no one of the steps given here can be accomplished independently of all others, following these steps can keep you on the right track.

Choose Your Subject

⁶ Sometimes you will be assigned a subject to write about. In this case, picking your subject means determining what angle or approach you will write from. As an example, you are assigned to write a paper on the life of Edgar Allan Poe. You still have considerable latitude in what you write about. You might make your paper an historical account of his life. Or you might make it an interpretative paper, mentioning only the high points of his life, then considering the possible effect each incident or event had on his personality, character, and subsequent life. Or you might organize your paper largely in terms of his writing, spending only a few paragraphs on his personal life, devoting most of your paper to an analysis and interpretation of the significance of his various literary works. There probably are many other approaches that you could take to the life of Edgar Allan Poe, each of which would constitute a report on his life, but which would be so different in character that each, in reality, would be on a different subject.

⁷ If you are given wide latitude in your choice of a subject, such as an essay on some topic in social science, some aspect of psychology, or some topic in botany on which to do research and write a report, picking your subject may present considerable problems of selection and elimination. Here are some guidelines that may help you make your decision.

⁸ First, *select a topic that you are interested in.* If you do a good job of preparing a paper, you will have to live with that paper for a good many hours. Choose a subject that holds sufficient interest for you that your research and writing become a matter of pursuing a genuine interest rather than the sheer drudgery of forcing yourself to concentrate on something of absolutely no interest to you.

⁹ *Pick a subject you already know something about.* Of course, if you are in a field where you know nothing about anything (this is rather hard to imagine, but sometimes college freshmen think they are in such a situation!), you may be forced to select a topic you know almost nothing about. In such an instance, you must start literally from the beginning in building up your knowledge. However, almost always you can find some acceptable topic that you already know enough about to be able

to visualize to some extent what preparing a report on it will involve. This, naturally, is a distinct advantage to you.

10   *Survey the library and other resources to determine whether sufficient material is available to enable you to prepare an adequate report on the subject you have chosen.* (Chapter Nine contains information on getting the most help from the library.) Do not depend on just the titles of books and articles; before finally determining the specific topic of your report, thumb through the books and articles to be sure that they actually contain the material you need in the necessary detail for your report. This also ensures that you have some knowledge of the area you intend to write about before irrevocably committing yourself to the topic you are considering. You may find that the subject you had tentatively selected is not at all what you really want to write on. Perhaps you had thought of this subject as encompassing one pattern of material, but you find that other writers, more experienced and knowledgeable than you, define the subject quite differently. Thus your preliminary survey clearly indicates that the subject, as conventionally conceived, is quite different from what you had anticipated and assumes a form you are not interested in. In this case, you select another topic and apply these same criteria to it. When you find one that satisfactorily meets the various criteria, you have picked your topic.

11   Do not cast aside this suggestion, thinking that you do not have time to spend in the library looking up information on a topic you may ultimately not even use. An hour's time spent checking through a topic idea and immediately discarding it is cheap insurance against spending ten hours—or twenty hours—on the topic, stubbornly holding on to it in spite of all the signposts indicating that this road will not lead to the outcome you desire. Conceivably, after spending many laborious hours you could make an acceptable paper from the topic. However, in most cases you will spend a great deal of time and will have a choice of two alternatives: discarding the topic, or knowing that you do not have enough material to make an adequate report.

12   Fourth, *choose a topic of a size appropriate to the length of paper and amount of time you have in mind.* College students customarily are expected to deal with a subject in greater depth than high school students are, and graduate students are expected to delve even deeper. Thus a freshman's term paper written in conjunction with a course in French, for example, would hardly be the place to attempt a treatise on "The French Revolution." The scope of this topic would be too big, both in terms of the amount of time that would be required and the number of pages necessary to include the degree of detail that a college professor usually expects of a student in a research paper.

"The Role of Danton in the French Revolution" might be a good possibility, or perhaps even "The Causes of the French Revolution," although this is getting rather broad, too, in view of the amount of detail you probably will be expected to include. "Foreign Influences That Contributed to the Causes of the French Revolution" is an example of how the subject of the causes of the French Revolution might be narrowed down to a topic more in keeping with the amount of time and number of words you propose to devote to the theme. The appropriateness of a subject in size and scope is very definitely one of the factors on which a teacher commonly grades a paper, so consider it well in your selection.

For her freshman history course, Sandy is required to write a term paper of about 3,000 words on some topic of American history. She runs through in her mind various possibilities— the Pilgrims, the Boston Tea Party, the Civil War, General Grant, Theodore Roosevelt, the California Gold Rush, and many others. None appeals to her. Finally she picks up her textbook and begins to look through the table of contents to see what else she might consider. She sees a subtitle, "The Slavery Issue." Aha! Better than wars or elections, Sandy thinks, and starts to work. After a couple of hours she decides to change her topic.

1. What are some reasons Sandy may have abandoned this topic?

Next Sandy tries looking through the index of her text for ideas. The name Nathan Hale catches her eye, and she recalls the story of the young Colonial schoolteacher who, captured by the British and about to be hanged as a spy, said, "I regret that I have but one life to give for my country." He sounds like an interesting person, so Sandy starts to work again, only to give up in about an hour.

2. Why do you suppose she abandoned Nathan Hale as the subject of her term paper?

Still searching, Sandy decides to fall back on something she feels sure she can handle—the administration of Franklin D. Roosevelt. After reading what her text has to say on the subject of his administration, she starts reading other accounts she locates in books in the library. She does not completely abandon her topic this time, but she does modify it somewhat. Finally she gets a very good term paper completed.

3. How and why could Sandy have changed her topic, "The Administration of President Franklin D. Roosevelt"?

4. List several alternative topics relating to Roosevelt that Sandy could have settled on as the subject of her term paper.

Gather Your Material

13   You can begin this process as a part of thumbing through library sources in your preliminary effort to determine the availability of sufficient material and the accuracy of your conception of the subject you have under consideration. By all means make notes of at least the location of material that impresses you as particularly important and worthwhile. Do not deliberately start the wholesale collection of material while you are still in the process of selecting your subject; doing so wastes your time. But do make notes of usable articles and chapters you encounter, saving yourself the unnecessary trouble of spending hours later on trying to locate an elusive reference that you remember but cannot relocate.

14   As students gain experience in library reasearch, a large percentage of them gradually develop the policy of noting on a card every reference checked, and making notes on the card of important ideas from that source. A page in a loose-leaf notebook can be used in place of a card if this is more convenient for you. The form you find most convenient may vary, but the habit is an invaluable one.

15   For a report suitable for a college course, instructors usually require that the researcher survey multiple references and sources of material rather than find one elaborate source and use it exclusively. When your biology professor, for example, instructs you to write a research paper on some biological subject, one of his purposes is to give you experience in locating and evaluating material from a number of different sources, and then synthesizing the facts and ideas drawn from multiple sources into one unified concept, which you present as your paper.

16   How much material should you gather before beginning to write your paper? How much material is properly expected of you for a college report? These questions cannot be answered dogmatically, but here are some considerations to help you answer them in light of your own specific situation. The steps discussed in this chapter suggest the logical sequence of beginning the various tasks involved in preparing a paper, but the accomplishment of each task commonly requires moving ahead to do a portion of more advanced steps in the preparation, then dropping back to fill gaps that have been revealed in earlier procedures—right up until the very last phase of preparing your report. Gathering material is not a step that you do once and for all, then turn your attention exclusively to other tasks.

17   As you gather your source materials, look for a pattern, an organization, an overall picture of your topic. When such a picture begins to form, you are ready to begin at least the first attempt at outlining your paper. As your outline becomes per-

fected, you can readily perceive whether you have collected enough material to complete a specific topic or subtopic. As you outline, and as you write your paper, you will constantly find it necessary to supplement the material you have gathered with additional facts and ideas and to substantiate your own ideas with facts and references derived from the writings of others. This is an example of the way the steps in preparing a written paper necessarily overlap.

[18] You should gather enough material that writing a paper of the length you are assigned becomes a matter of selecting and discarding rather than stretching and padding to cover the required number of pages. You should gather enough data that your paper represents a reasonable sample of what a number of different authorities have thought and written, and an acquaintance with not one or two, but a variety of points of view. You should gather enough material that a list of your sources (included as footnotes and bibliography) testifies that you have in actuality done research on the subject, not merely read what two or three people wrote on it. You should gather enough material that your paper represents a synthesis of a variety of materials, viewpoints, and approaches, and not merely a book report on one or a few closely related reference sources. As a final criterion, you should gather as much material as your time permits, as long as additional research continues to bring forth new facts, ideas, or approaches that vary significantly from the ones you already have.

[19] Begin the actual writing of your paper as early as you reasonably can. It is likely that ten college students find they have gathered information and postponed beginning to write their papers until uncomfortably late for every one student who begins writing earlier in the process of gathering material than he should have done. You may take this as a warning.

[20] A word to the wise is perhaps in order. It is entirely possible that you are as intelligent and perceptive as your professor. However, the likelihood of your having as wide an acquaintance as he has with the works in the field in which he is teaching is extremely remote. He has spent some years doing exactly what you are doing now, and it is very likely that at some time he has researched the same topic you are now working on. Therefore, when time is running short and you encounter an article or some other write-up of your subject in some remote source, resist the temptation to say, "Aha! I have it! I will copy this and he will never know that I took it verbatim from a published work!" It is unlikely that he will be fooled by such a device. In the first place, the chances are good that no matter how remote the source seems to you, he will be familiar with it. In the second place, the chances of his believing that you, an undergraduate, wrote a

research paper of a quality that would be published in a scholarly or professional journal or similar publication is equally remote, unless you are a genuinely outstanding student—in which case you do not need to copy someone else's work.

21 Equally dangerous is the venture some students have tried of using a paper written by a former student in a previous course or year. To be perfectly frank, you sometimes get away with this. However, through reading hundreds and thousands of papers, professors develop an uncanny knack for recalling a phrase, an unusual use of a word, or some distinguishing characteristic that sparks in their mind a dim memory of another paper. Once this happens and they begin to consciously search their memory, the game is up. A certain percentage of times you might get away with it—but it may take only one instance of being caught to blight or terminate your college career. Do not run this risk.

Outline the Paper

22 The principles and procedures for outlining a written paper do not differ significantly from the procedures suggested for outlining material to be presented as an oral report. You determine the principal points of your report and gather the material that relates logically to each point. Your written report may or may not have clearly identifiable topic headings corresponding to the main points of an oral report, depending on your preference and the type of paper you are writing. If it is a research paper, the topic headings probably are a good idea. In some other types of compositions topic headings are seldom used. Whether or not topic heads are used in your final form, be sure to make a detailed written outline, in which your different topics are clearly identified and the material to be included under each topic is outlined, point by point, to guide you in your writing.

23 It is not at all unusual for an experienced researcher or writer to prepare a half-dozen outlines before perfecting one that fully meets his own criteria of suitability and logic and at the same time comprehensively and satisfactorily organizes the material that he plans to include in his report. Do not be afraid, therefore, to prepare several outlines before beginning to write your paper. A final outline, which will guide you through your subject in a clear, logical, and comprehensive manner, saves hours of rewriting to eliminate errors in organization.

24 At this stage of preparing a paper, you will frequently find that you need to change your subject slightly, or even drastically. As you begin to see in black and white the shape that your material is taking, you may find that it suggests a different emphasis as more appropriate than the one you started with. If you have

To Prepare a Good Written Report . . .

Research   Write   Research Further

Write   Edit and Rewrite

been assigned a specific topic to write on, this may necessitate rethinking your material to give it proper emphasis. On the other hand, if you are permitted to choose your own subject, you may find it desirable to simply alter your subject to represent your more mature thinking rather than attempting to make the material you have gathered and the organization it suggests conform to the aspect of the subject that you originally selected. There is nothing at all wrong in changing your subject to fit your material and the organization that seems desirable to you. As a matter of fact, many graduate students working on elaborate research projects find that a redefinition of their topic is indicated by the trend of their data and by analysis of the material they have collected.

25   Remember that if you do change your subject you must carefully scrutinize the title of your paper to be sure that, with this new turn it has taken, the contents are accurately described by the title. A very fine paper is considerably less acceptable if it does not tell the reader what the title leads him to expect.

Write Your Paper

26   It is a good idea to double-space the first draft of your paper, whether you type it or write it in longhand. This allows room for making editorial changes and adding ideas which, upon rereading, you find will suitably fit in a certain place. Whether you write the entire paper, working completely through your outline be-

fore beginning scrutiny of the separate parts of what you have written, or whether you examine it paragraph by paragraph as you proceed, is largely a matter of individual taste and preference.

27 The care you have taken in drawing up a logical, comprehensive outline leads you to write the right things in the right order and helps you avoid rambling or becoming incoherent. Try to say what you have to say clearly and in a straightforward manner. Avoid writing long, involved sentences, drifting off the subject, bringing in irrelevant material, and becoming unduly wordy. At this stage of preparation, the big job is to get your ideas down on paper, following the guidance of your outline to ensure comprehensive coverage.

28 *Begin writing your paper as early as you can.* Some research papers perhaps cannot be begun until all data are completely analyzed, but they are rare exceptions. Writing portions of the paper before preparation of all material is complete usually is both possible and desirable. To postpone writing until all preliminary work is complete almost guarantees a frantic scramble to get the paper finished on time, a poorly written paper, or, most probable of all, both! In twenty years of dealing with students who were writing papers of significant complexity, the author has never encountered one who said that the actual writing and editing of a major paper took less time than he had anticipated. Almost 100 per cent find that it takes substantially longer than they originally expected.

Edit for Content and Organization

29 To edit means to examine material critically to see if its content, manner of expression, and grammatical construction are as nearly perfect as possible. If there is one secret of preparing a superior composition, research report, or other similar written exercise, perhaps it is this: meticulous editing and re-editing of what you write. Professional writers, men and women who make their living by their pens, habitually read and reread, scrutinize, weigh each word, check each sentence, to polish their product to the finest possible point. On the other hand, it is most difficult to get amateur writers to accept the importance of this repeated editing. The inexperienced person customarily seems to feel that one or at the very most two rather perfunctory readings of what he has written are all that should be necessary.

30 Many people who have worked at teaching intelligent, well-educated adults to improve their writing have found that simply persuading them to carefully and critically read and re-read what they have written largely accomplishes the desired improvement of quality of writing. In this chapter we are exploring a number of techniques for making your written papers

the best that you possibly can. Do not forget that although you can never produce a paper that is better than its content, your paper will also be no better than the quantity and quality of editing and re-editing that you have devoted to perfecting the presentation of your ideas.

31   Having double-spaced your draft makes it easier for you to find convenient space to write in corrections after deleting offending words or sentences, or to add material that you perceive on closer inspection to fall more appropriately at another point. Any clear system that you may select to show that a sentence or paragraph should be moved from one place to another is satisfactory—asterisks, lines running from the sentence to its new placement, or marginal notes. An asterisk and the word *Over*, indicating an insertion of new material which you have written on the back of the sheet, is also a timesaving device; it enables you to make major additions to what you have written with a minimum of rewriting or confusion.

32   Read your paper through slowly and carefully. Read it more slowly and with greater attention to detail than you give to a reading assignment, because in reading an assignment all you are trying to do is clearly grasp and interpret the ideas of the author. In editing a paper, you are reading not only to grasp the ideas but also to see if they are clearly expressed and if they are the ideas that should be included. You are also reading to see if each idea is included in the place where it will be most effective, and to see if the facts and ideas interlock firmly and naturally to compose a tight, logically progressive development of your thought rather than just a loose collection of sentences. Among the specific areas you should pay special attention to as you critically review the content of your paper are the four discussed in the following paragraphs.

33   *Accuracy of Facts and Substantiating Statements.* Often, in the enthusiasm of writing, a person gets carried away and makes generalizations that are too broad, overstates his case, records as fact some general impression he has gained, or expresses a perfectly legitimate statement in such a manner that it gives a wrong impression. In this critical reading you should check to be sure that you have not fallen into one of these traps.

34   In eliminating what seems to be unnecessary detail in the process of writing, a person may retain a conclusion that does not actually follow from the details he included in his paper. Your statements and conclusions should be carefully checked during this reading to see that you have not made unwarranted generalizations or included material that requires substantiation to tie it into your general topic or to demonstrate its veracity and validity. Determining whether your statements have the necessary

substantiation is not too difficult a task. As you read, merely ask yourself the question: "Does what I am saying here stand on its own feet, not requiring proof or substantiation, or does it call for further explanation?"

35 *Citing References and Sources.* In much or most of the writing you will be expected to do in college, you will be required to identify the authority for certain statements and the source of certain facts. The proper use and form of footnotes, bibliographical references, etc., is too extensive and too technical for a book of this sort. The titles of several widely used books on this and other subjects related to writing that will give you authoritative, detailed rules regarding documentation are included at the end of this chapter. The purpose here is to call your attention to different areas that you must scrutinize thoughtfully in your writing, and to give broad suggestions as to how to accomplish your editing.

36 There is no formal rule as to what statements need to be documented and what material can be included in a written report without further corroboration. Obviously, if you quote more than a single phrase (or even one phrase, if it is a unique or distinctive one), professional courtesy and good writing procedures require that you cite the source of your statement. It is obviously impractical to cite sentence by sentence, or even paragraph by paragraph, the source of *all* your information, although your professor may require that as an exercise in learning the proper method of using footnotes, references, and bibliography, you cite sources of information more fully than you normally would.

37 There are two basic criteria for citing references: (1) quoting verbatim from the writings or speeches of an individual, or presenting his precise views or findings requires that you extend him the courtesy of acknowledging his contribution; (2) presenting a fact that is obscure or not well known requires that you cite the original source to attest its authenticity. Thus, if you found one writer mentioning some particular of Ponce de Leon's explorations, but found no reference to it anywhere else in your research, identification of your source of information is advisable if you refer to this fact.

38 *Adequacy of Facts and Presentation.* During this thoughtful reading for content, you should also review your outline for the paper, recalling all the information that you gathered, to determine whether you have covered enough ground and included enough detail to constitute an adequate treatment of your subject. What constitutes adequate discussion and facts will vary according to your audience. You must consider the scope of each topic and make a judgment as to the degree of detail appropriate to the objective of your report and to the nature of your particular audience. Your criterion for this may be your knowledge of the amount of detail and degree of comprehensiveness expected by the professor for whom you are writing the report, or it may be the degree of detail you feel will be of interest to some other audience. A mental check of what you have written against the mass of information you gathered on each topic and subpoint, and a decision as to whether what you have included represents comprehensively enough the general thought of other writers in the field, gives you a standard for determining the adequacy, both in scope and depth, of your own paper.

39   *Organization.* A well-written paper is easy for a reader to follow. He sees how each sentence and paragraph contributes to the overall purpose of the paper and how each fits into the context of the report as a whole. Ideas related to a given topic are included in conjunction with that topic. Think of your facts and ideas as a jigsaw puzzle: Every piece must be at the right spot to contribute to the overall picture that is being formed. If you formulated a good outline and followed it well, perfecting the organization of the full text of your report should be little trouble.

40   You can profitably keep three factors in mind when checking the organization of your paper. (1) Coherence: Are your sentences saying something? Do they fit together so that they give the reader an understanding of the topic? (2) Sequence: Does the natural pattern of thought or fact on a subject emerge from the order in which you have presented your material? Do your thoughts follow in clear succession, each thought or sentence being at the point where it logically belongs in the report? (3) Paragraphing: Does each paragraph deal with one, and only one, topic?

Edit for Composition and Grammatical Construction

41   Very few people can edit a paper simultaneously for content and organization and for composition and grammatical construction. Probably no one can do so without a great deal of experience in such editing, simply because there are more points to look for than the amateur can check in one reading. After you are satisfied that the content is both accurate and complete and the organization clear and logical, read your paper again, this time not thinking primarily about its content but watching for errors in sentence construction or composition. It is quite within the prerogative of any professor, of any subject, to require that grammatical construction in written work submitted to him be technically correct. Therefore, you should read your paper with

meticulous attention to all grammatical principles and usages. Errors commonly found in papers of college students are given below.

42 *Incomplete Sentences.* It is amazing how frequently a person who is absorbed in his thoughts and his subject matter will write what he thinks is a sentence but, in actuality, will omit the subject or the verb. Instead of a sentence, he has a meaningless collection of words that do not say anything. Here is a typical example of a sentence without a verb: "The ancestor of our horse, the eohippus, the size of a small dog and having three toes on each hind foot and four on each front foot, during the lower Eocene epoch in the western United States." Simply reading each sentence critically to see if it actually is a complete sentence and transmits a complete thought will enable you to avoid this common error in your paper.

43 *Disagreement in Number of Subject and Verb.* This is another of the most frequent errors made by college students. For example, "The task faced by France, Italy, and Germany following World War II of rebuilding an economy, re-establishing a stable social order, and converting once more to a peacetime climate were stupendous." Here the writer has either thought of "France, Italy, and Germany" or "rebuilding . . . re-establishing . . . converting" as the subject, or has overlooked having written the real subject as "task," not "tasks." It is natural to make such errors when writing, but it is not permissible to fail to detect them before handing in the paper.

44 *Incorrect Case of Pronouns.* Adherence to traditional rules of grammar admittedly has been relaxed considerably in the past few years. Some professors will not count as an error such expressions as "It is me," or "She was in class with he and I," but such usages are errors, and a college report should be written in scholarly language. Errors in the case of pronouns following prepositions seem to be most frequent. "The greatest contribution made by he and his associates . . ." is grammatically incorrect, and no amount of professional tolerance can keep it from being bad writing.

45 Of course, to follow these admonitions, you have to know more than a smattering of English grammar. If you find yourself confused or lacking the technical knowledge to apply the rules, either register immediately for a remedial course in English or get one of the books dealing with principles of grammatical usage listed at the end of this chapter, study at least one such book, and then use it as a constant reference in preparing every piece of written work you are to turn in.

46 *Errors in Punctuation.* To give even the broadest direction in the use of punctuation marks is beyond the scope of this book. Again, use one of the references cited at the end of this chapter and keep it beside you as you write, making frequent reference to it whenever you are uncertain as to proper punctuation. In your editing, read a sentence and see whether, within the sentence, there is need to redirect the reader's thought from one path to another. If so, you need some punctuation. Check your manual to see what and how.

47 *Misspellings.* This is by all odds the most frequent and the most nearly inexcusable of errors found in papers submitted by college students. An occasional misspelling may be tolerable, although undesirable, on an examination (where obviously a dictionary is not available) if a student wishes to use a word he is not accustomed to writing to express his thoughts with maximum clarity. A misspelled word in a report written outside class is well-nigh inexcusable. and you will find that most of your professors, whether in English or embryology, subscribe wholeheartedly to this view. It immediately identifies the writer as a careless person who has not devoted sufficient time and care to the preparation of his report.

48 Keep a dictionary beside you while writing, and whenever you start to use a word you are not certain how to spell, verify its spelling by your dictionary. If this means that you must spend a great deal of time in looking up words, prepare to spend that time; your education in this area thus far has been neglected, and it is time you achieved the mastery of your mother tongue that a college student is supposed to have.

49 In your editing, be even more meticulous about looking up the spelling of any word that you are not thoroughly familiar with: Check to see if a word has two *l*'s or one, two *s*'s or one, a final *e;* to see if *i* comes before *e;* if an *a* or an *e* is correct. These kinds of errors are extremely frequent, but to list even the common errors encountered in students' spelling is to explore the absolute limits of human ingenuity—misapplied. Making absolutely certain that your spelling is absolutely perfect may be time consuming, but it is a simple thing that anyone can do if he merely takes the time and pains. Thus, failure to do so is to automatically convict yourself of carelessness and lack of concern over preparing an acceptable paper. Your professor will evaluate your effort accordingly.

50 *Rambling Sentences.* It is easy to be following a thought while writing, let your sentence wander into a closely related thought, and, being absorbed in your subject, continue to link thought after thought into one sentence, which is bad composition but can be easily detected in editing, and this is a representative example of a rambling sentence, but they are among the easiest grammatical errors to detect, since they stand out like sore thumbs if subjected to even perfunctory editing, and can be rewritten as several sentences. Do it.

Write a Second Draft of Your Paper

51 In the long run, it probably will save you time to prepare the corrected version of your paper in what hopefully would be final form to turn in. Many times subsequent editing will require enough changes to necessitate writing the paper a third time. You will frequently find, however, that with care, although some pages of your report may have to be written a third time, many pages of your second version can be used, with the rewritten (or retyped) pages.

52 If you have done an excellent job in the preceding two steps (editing your paper critically both for content and organization and for composition and grammatical construction), you will find that often, especially as your skill in writing and editing develops, this second typing or writing can qualify as the final copy. Most professors are quite reasonable about permitting papers to be turned in with inserted notes and corrections made neatly by typewriter or pen. Certainly, they are much more toler-

Read Critically to Correct Errors and Improve Sentence Structure

ant of such slight defacements of a page than they are of errors that you have not detected and corrected. Read over your second draft carefully—for content, for composition and grammar, and for typing or writing errors. An invariable rule to follow before submitting any paper as your finished product is this: Always read critically at least one time every line of every page that you have written!

At the end of the class period today Virgil got back his first theme submitted in freshman English. He received a "C" on it. He is both disappointed and angry, for he had worked hard on that paper. His first impulse was to go back into the room and demand that the teacher tell him what was wrong with it. As it happened, however, the teacher was surrounded by other students, and Virgil knew that he would not have time to stop and wait his turn and still get to his next class on time.

In his room after supper Virgil again picked up the paper. He wondered how he might get a better idea of what was wrong with this paper and how he could do better on his theme due next week.

1. How might Virgil determine what qualities the professor was looking for in a composition?

2. How might Virgil acquire a clearer idea of what was wrong with his theme without demanding an explanation from the professor? List as many ways as you can.

References

Arntson, Dorothy H. *Beginning College Writing*. Chicago: Scott, Foresman, 1963.

Cohen, Bernard B. *Writing About Literature*. Chicago: Scott, Foresman, 1963.

Estrin, Herman A. *Technical and Professional Writing:* A Practical Anthology. New York: Harcourt, Brace & World, 1963.

Ives, Sumner, and Stephen O. Mitchell. *Language, Style, Ideas*. New York: Harcourt, Brace & World, 1964.

Knickerbocker, Kenneth L. *Ideas for Writing*, 3rd ed. New York: Holt, Rinehart & Winston, 1962.

Levin, Gerald H. *Prose Models*. New York: Harcourt, Brace & World, 1964.

McCrimmon, James M. *Writing with a Purpose,* 3rd ed. Boston: Houghton Mifflin, 1963.

McDonnell, Robert F., and William E. Morris. *Form and Focus.* New York: Harcourt, Brace & World, 1964.

Perrin, Porter G., rev. by Karl W. Dykema and Wilma R. Ebbitt. *Writer's Guide and Index to English,* 4th ed. Chicago: Scott, Foresman, 1965.

Sams, Henry W., and Waldo F. McNeir, eds. *Problems in Reading and Writing.* Englewood Cliffs, N.J.: Prentice-Hall, 1949.

Warnock, Robert. *Using Good English, Form C,* ed. Porter G. Perrin and Harrison G. Plott, Jr. Chicago: Scott, Foresman, 1958.

After PREVIEWING this chapter, write your summary paragraph here.

GETTING HELP FROM THE LIBRARY

1   When you need any sort of information not included in one of your textbooks, the library is the first place to look for it. Only if you cannot find it there should you spend the extra time and effort required to seek it out from other sources. If you want information about the amount of flax used in the United States last year, you undoubtedly could get it by writing your congressman, the U.S. Department of Agriculture, or perhaps the Library of Congress, but you probably can get it more quickly and easily from one of the yearbooks or almanacs in your own college library. If you have never put a college library to the test of locating specialized information, you have no idea how many resources a librarian has for helping you find the material you need!

2   Even when you are studying a textbook assignment on a given topic, it is often profitable to check some library source on the same topic. You may find a more condensed version of the theme you are studying that will give you the perspective, the broad, general picture you need in order to organize and assimilate the details your text presents on the topic. Or, on the other hand, you may find a reference that gives you details that supplement and clarify the too brief treatment of the subject in your textbook that left you not quite understanding what it was all about. Or, perhaps the writer of the reference you find in the library will express things in a manner that you understand more readily than you did the exposition in the text. In short, if the treatment of a topic in the textbook leaves you baffled or puzzled, you probably can find clarification in the library.

Divisions of a Library

3   The first step in learning to use your library easily and well is to *preview* the library. Look it over to see what is there and familiarize yourself with where things are. Begin by finding, or asking a librarian to direct you to, a floor plan of the library. (If your college library is so small you can easily walk through each section of it and see what is there, you do not need to do this, of course. In big libraries, however, there are so many floors and rooms that you will need a map to learn your way around.) Ask for any directions on the use of the library that have been published for students. While this chapter will give you a good introduction to the use of college libraries generally, a descrip-

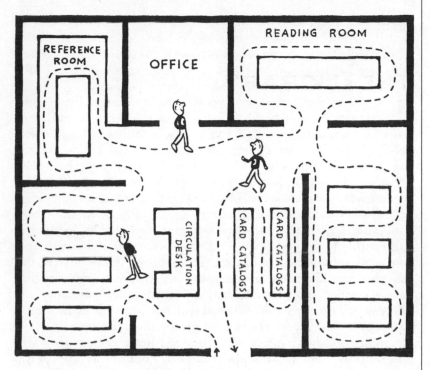

REFERENCE ROOM

OFFICE

READING ROOM

CIRCULATION DESK

CARD CATALOGS

CARD CATALOGS

Browse Through the Library

tion and instructions prepared specifically for your own college library can tell you much more. Use of such instructions can save you literally hours in locating information you want. Study the floor plan to see the different sections of the library; then walk through them, looking at the books and periodicals to get a general idea of what each section contains. Most college libraries will be divided into the following three basic major divisions, and the larger libraries will have others also.

Reference Room

[4] Here you will find encyclopedias, dictionaries, indexes (books listing articles on given topics that have appeared in magazines of various types), bibliographies, biographical directories, atlases, directories of all kinds—in short, all types of compilations of specialized categories of information. In general, encyclopedias give you relatively brief coverage of subjects, a mere summary of knowledge or of a branch of knowledge. An unabridged dictionary, which you will find in the reference room, not only gives you proper spellings, pronunciations, and definitions, but also often will direct your mind to related aspects of a subject that had not occurred to you. You will also find specialized dictionaries devoted to specific areas—psychology,

biology, and other fields. Bibliographies and indexes direct you to still further information on given subjects or authors, and the more specialized reference books contain more detailed information. The librarian can help you determine which source would be most likely to contain the information you seek.

5   If you want information on college fraternities in the United States, you will find a book on them in the reference room. If you want to locate articles dealing with automobile accidents, there will be a guide to periodical literature that will list such published articles and tell you what issue of what magazine contained each article listed. When you are unable to find the type of reference book you need or you do not know what reference book would be most likely to contain the information you need, ask the librarian or desk assistant for help. Probably she will be able to suggest several references for you. If, for instance, you want information about recent advances in chemistry, she can give you an index telling you where to locate articles that have appeared in popular magazines, and another index that will tell you what articles on this subject have appeared in which issues of technical, scholarly, and professional journals.

6   Time used to inspect your college library's reference room will be time well spent. Walk around it. Look at the titles of the books on the shelves. If the title of a book your eyes fall upon does not immediately identify to you what the book is about, pick up the book and glance through it. Doing this gives you a better "feel" of the reference room, what it is really like and what it contains, than you could obtain through hours of simply reading books on the use of the library.

Periodical Room

7   By definition a periodical is a publication that appears at regular intervals. The periodical room, therefore, is the room where you will find newspapers, magazines, and journals. The newspapers may be the same ones you have been accustomed to reading, as well as others from different cities or sections of the country. The magazines, however, are a different matter. Walk along the shelves where they are displayed and read their titles. In even a small college library you will find dozens of magazines you did not know existed. In a large library there will be literally hundreds of titles strange to you. There may be few of the magazines you see on a newsstand—the "popular" magazines. You may look in vain for most of those you have enjoyed reading. This is because the college library is intended primarily to afford research facilities in various academic areas and to provide highly technical and specialized information on thought and developments in the various arts and sciences, not to offer material for your entertainment or general reading. (Many colleges

do have a "recreational reading room" where popular magazines and current fiction can be found, but this is often apart from the main periodical room.)

8 The bulk of magazines in a college library's periodical room are of the sort called "technical, professional, and scholarly journals." They are filled with articles by scholars in the academic field represented by the journal, often articles that require advanced study in order to be read with understanding. These journals are the media by which new ideas, theories, discoveries, and research results in a specific field—chemistry, English, history, sociology, and all others—are disseminated by scholars to all their colleagues.

9 From time to time you will be assigned articles to read in some of these journals. In most libraries current issues are arranged alphabetically on the shelves. Issues for approximately the last year are usually on adjacent shelves. Earlier issues are bound in chronological order in book form and stored in a special section of the library, or are available on microfilm. Some colleges permit students to go into the stacks (the levels where the bulk of the library's volumes are kept) and look for the book they want. Others require sutdents to fill out a card asking for a particular volume and give it to a desk assistant, who obtains the volume and brings it to the student. Ordinarily, neither books from the reference room nor bound periodicals can be checked out of the library; they must be used in the reading rooms provided.

10 Also in the periodical room you will find dozens of "special interest" magazines. Many of these are sent free to the library as a public relations measure by the organizations publishing them. You may find a magazine on the lumber industry in the Northwest, one devoted exclusively to the merchandise and work of the door-to-door salesman, and a dozen published by religious denominations. Usually these magazines are not bound but are discarded after they are a year or so old.

The Stacks

11 The stacks make up the bulk of the library. This is the place where most of the books are kept, as well as the bound journals already mentioned. In most libraries there will be floor after floor of stacks, which may or may not be open to the student depending on the prevailing college policy. Every one of the thousands of books that the library stacks contain has its own special place on the shelves so that you or the librarian can quickly lay your hands on the exact book you want. The numbers and letters you see on the spines of the books indicate the subject arcas the books fall into and are the basis for the filing system almost all libraries use for arranging books in their stacks.

The Card Catalog

¹² Aside from the librarian, who is the final authority on what is in the library and where to find it, the most useful device for locating a book or reference is the card catalog. Usually the card catalog is found in or immediately adjacent to the main entrance to the "working" portion of the library, convenient to the main desk where books are checked out. The card catalog is made up of a bank of filing cabinets, each composed of many small drawers containing file cards. In a large library there will be row after row of cabinets full of these little drawers, each filled with cards designating books.

¹³ The card catalog customarily contains at least two sections, one labeled "Author and Title Index" and the other "Subject Index." All authors whose books (but not journal articles, necessarily) the library owns, and the titles of these volumes, will be filed in one alphabetical arrangement in the "Author and Title" section of the card catalog. All books written by a particular author that are owned by the library will be listed under his name. In addition to enabling you to locate a specific book by using the name of its author, you will find the "Author and Title Index" especially helpful if you want to study a particular author intensively.

¹⁴ In the "Subject Index" of the card catalog you may locate a book by the subject with which it deals. Properly placed alphabetically in this bank of files will be a section titled "History," for example, and under it will be subsections on the various areas of history—"American," "Asiatic," "religious," "Spanish," and so on—on which the library contains volumes. This makes it possible for you to locate all the books on a given subject in the library even if you do not know the titles of the books or their authors. You simply look for the subject you are seeking books on and run through the cards under that section in the card catalog. Each card will contain the title of a book related to that area, its author, and a very brief description of the contents of the book. From this you can select books that seem to meet your particular need, even though you did not know in advance any author or the title of any specific book that would answer your purpose.

¹⁵ Every book in the library will be listed on at least two different cards in the card catalog. It will be filed alphabetically according to its title and according to its author's surname. In all probability it also will be filed under at least one subject category in the "Subject Index." There may be more than one subject card for a book—for example, a book may be listed under both "American history" and "New England history."

¹⁶ Whether it is filed by subject, title, or author, the card

representing a book in the card catalog will contain the same information about the book: the publisher, date of publication, number of pages, and usually a brief description of what it is about. But the key to locating a book in the library lies in the set of numbers you will find in the upper left corner of the card. These numbers, which usually consist of two or three lines and include the first letter of the author's name, are the "call number" of the book. The book is shelved in the stacks by its call number, following a plan used by almost all college libraries in the United States and called the "Dewey decimal system." (A few libraries use the Library of Congress catalog system.)

17   In the Dewey decimal system of cataloging, the first three digits of the number (upper left) indicate the general subject area of the book—philosophy, fine arts, pure science, and so on. The numbers on the same line following the decimal indicate what subsection of the general subject the book falls under—in the case of the pure science listing, for instance, they will show whether the book is on chemistry, mathematics, etc., and more specifically, whether it treats organic chemistry or some other subclassification. The letter commonly found at the beginning of the second line of the call number is the first letter of the author's surname, and the remaining numbers fix even more exactly the position of the book in the stacks. Libraries vary in the amount of information they require you to furnish about a book that you wish the desk assistant or librarian to locate for you, but ordinarily unless otherwise instructed you should fill out a "call card" giving the complete call number of the book, the name of the author, and the exact title of the book.

18   If a librarian is to locate the book for you and finds it is not immediately available, she will tell you the reason. If you are to enter the stacks and look up the book for yourself, do not stop if you cannot find it. Make out a "call card" and tell the librarian that you cannot find the book, and ask her help. The book may be in the stacks but out of its proper place; the librarian, with years of experience in locating misplaced books, can find it better than you can. She can check the circulation file to see if the book is checked out, and when it is due to be returned. You may be able to arrange to be called when it is returned or have it held for you. It may be unexplainably missing, or at the bindery for rebinding. Or, it may be on reserve—that is, placed by a professor in a restricted area for use by students in his courses, and therefore taken from its usual place in the stacks and kept with other reserve books for quick access.

Taking Notes on Library Books

19   When you are reading from a reference book in the library, or from a book one of your teachers has placed on the reserve

shelf there, you will probably think that you will easily and accurately remember most of what you read. At the time, the material may seem quite simple to you, or will appear to be such an important or profound concept that you are sure you will remember it. But chances are that as time passes, what you read in the library will become fuzzy in your mind or even fade from it. If it fades from your memory, you have in large measure wasted the time you spent reading it. If it becomes so fuzzy as to require you to retrace your steps to the library and look it up and reread it, you have needlessly spent time you could have used either more profitably or pleasurably. This is the reason it is important that you take notes on material you read in the library or on library books that you cannot retain permanently in your room.

20   The mechanics of taking notes on library books differ little from the principles for note-taking discussed in Chapter Four. In two important respects, however, you will encounter necessary changes of what may be your routine method of taking notes. First, obviously all notes on library books must be recorded on your file cards or in your notebook, not on the margins of the page. Second, notes taken from a library book or journal should be carefully identified as to *source*. Take one extra minute to jot down in your notebook the author, title, and call number of a book or issue of a periodical you are reading, and add the page numbers of the material on which your notes were taken. A surprising number of times, for some completely unpredictable reason, you will need to refer again to the source of your notes. Although when you are writing the notes you feel you could not possibly forget where they are from, you probably will forget, especially when you must read and take notes from several different sources. In many instances, especially if you are writing a paper on the subject of your reading, you will be required to identify the references from which your information was gained.

21   People with the most extensive experience in library research almost invariably take their notes on 3×5 or 4×6 cards, one reference to a card, with cards numbered 1, 2, 3, . . ., if more than one card is required for a single reference. There is no real reason why a loose-leaf notebook could not be used satisfactorily instead of cards, one reference to a page, but do not use a bound notebook. Inevitably you will want to add to notes on some references and have no room to do so, or will have to paw through many pages to find the particular reference you want, since you cannot keep references in a bound notebook alphabetically. File your reference cards, or pages in your loose-leaf notebook, in alphabetical order, by title or by author as best suits your purposes, and you will be able to find your notes on a given reference quickly. Keep your reference cards in a small box, or held

together by a rubber band, so they always will be together and not scattered haphazardly here and there.

²² The suggestions in this chapter, plus the published directions for use of your particular college library, which most libraries issue to students, will enable you to use the library efficiently. The cardinal rules to remember are: (1) Know what is in your library and get in the habit of using the library for every bit of help it affords you in your schoolwork. (2) Ask a librarian or desk assistant for help when for any reason you are unable to locate information you need. Even if the reference you need is not in your library, she often can arrange an interlibrary loan if it is really important for you to have access to the volume.

1. List as many library sources as you can think of from which you might locate information on General Douglas MacArthur.

2. Name all the library sources you can think of through which you might reasonably expect to locate information on the sponge industry of Tarpon Springs, Florida.

After PREVIEWING this chapter, write your summary paragraph here.

PREPARING
A BETTER
EXAMINATION PAPER

[1] Good examination grades begin with good study throughout a course. If you follow the R.S.V.P. procedure of study, you should have little to worry about on that score. In addition to your basic study, however, your examination grades will be influenced markedly by how well you review for and take the examination. This chapter tells you how to do both, with maximum returns for the effort you expend.

Preparing for an Examination

[2] No matter how thoroughly you study your daily assignments, a thorough review just before an examination is an absolute necessity if you are to make the grades your study deserves. You cover a tremendous amount of material during a course, and you probably are taking from three to six courses. Over a period of weeks or months, the keenest memory of details and ideas of a course is blunted. The clear picture of a topic that you developed in your R.S.V.P. procedure of study becomes a bit blurred as you study literally hundreds of other assignments. So, the last day (or two or three, if your examination schedule permits) before examination, give your course a thorough and comprehensive review. The process will bring back into keen focus the things you learned in your original study of each assignment, and your notes, which you corrected to reflect your instructor's explanations and discussion in the class period, will put you in top shape to reach new highs in your examination grades.

Review, but Do Not Cram

[3] Do as much last minute reviewing as you can, but do not cram. There is all the difference in the world between reviewing and cramming. Cramming is a frantic attempt to stuff one's mind as full as possible of facts and ideas within and for a short time. Review is a re-examination of familiar material to clarify one's understanding, refresh one's memory, and pick up any important material that has been overlooked or has slipped out of mind. The crammer reads, reads, reads, trying doggedly and desperately to cover in a single night everything he should have learned in an entire term. Typically he tries to semi-memorize facts and concepts which hazy memories lead him to fear are important,

or as many indiscriminate facts as possible. Like an inept swimmer threshing wildly in the water, he reads furiously, often moving his lips in an effort to force the words into his mind, trying to compensate by violence of concentration for his lack of comprehension of what he is supposed to be doing.

4   Not so the reviewer. He thinks about what he is studying. He may profitably use a modified R.S.V.P. procedure in reviewing. Glancing at his marginal note beside a paragraph, he gets an idea of the essence of the paragraph, as he did earlier by PRE-VIEWING it. This time, having once used the R.S.V.P. procedure on the paragraph and thus having grasped its significance, he does not need to STUDY the paragraph again. With the marginal note to cue him, he proceeds to VERBALIZE the content of the paragraph. Then he rapidly scans the paragraph to see if his reconstruction of it is correct. (This is important. Sometimes you may think you know a topic thoroughly when you really do not. By scanning the material as you review, you not only *know* that you know it, you also refresh your mind on it again.) Quite logically, then, reviewing for an examination becomes a process essentially the same as the REVIEW step of the R.S.V.P. procedure.

5   If the reviewer did overlook something important in his VERBALIZING of the paragraph, he makes a mental note to be sure to include that item in any future consideration of the topic. If he did not, he determines the answer to the question, "How does this fit into the overall subject?" and proceeds to the next

Review   Don't Cram

paragraph. The result: After two—or ten—hours of study, he has systematically reconsidered the material of his course, strengthened any weak spots, and gained a new appreciation of the construction of the whole subject in the process. This is reviewing! It results in a clear, comprehensive mental picture of the material reviewed, whereas cramming too frequently produces a buzzing, phantasmagoric confusion. The efficient reviewer follows the same principles in reviewing lecture notes. Taking his cue from the heading of a major point, he VERBALIZES the content of the point, then checks with his more detailed notes to verify or correct his memory.

Give Special Attention to Material the Professor Emphasized

6   The purpose of an examination is to measure the extent to which students learned the more important facts and concepts of the subject covered. Therefore, your professor will ask most questions on topics that he considers most important. Almost certainly he will have spent more class time on these important topics than on less important ones, and if you followed the suggestions of the R.S.V.P. system and recorded through lecture and marginal notes the points he emphasized in his lectures, you can identify easily the topics most likely to be covered on the examination.

7   Of course, an instructor does not want you to study a relatively small number of major points with such fierce intensity that you neglect the general body of the subject. Do not rely exclusively on "spotting" questions that seem likely to appear on examinations and concentrate on them to the exclusion of thorough, comprehensive study. The chances are that the instructor will ask some questions about some topics other than those he considers most crucial. Therefore, a good rule of thumb is this: Make certain you know everything that the professor particularly emphasized, and learn the remainder as well as you can.

8   At this point the student who listened thoughtfully to lectures and efficiently employed the procedures for effective listening set forth in Chapter Four reaps the full reward of his forethought. You can see that the accuracy with which you note the topics of special importance in the professor's lectures during the course may have an important bearing on the marks you make on tests and examinations. Effective review for examinations really starts with judicious use of your mind and pencil when studying your textbook and during class periods—use them both to keep a permanent record of the topics of greatest importance in the course. Noting important ideas with both your mind and

your pencil will mean extra points for you when review time and examinations come.

Formulate Questions About Important Topics and Think Them Through

⁹ A good variation on the practice of VERBALIZING paragraphs from your notes, or a good supplement to this technique, is the practice of formulating a question about a topic, then VERBALIZING the best answer to it, as discussed in the section of Chapter Seven dealing with preparing to answer questions in class. Consider, for instance, the establishment of the Federal Reserve Bank. Depending on the course you are taking and the aspect most stressed by your instructor, or both, an examination question about this institution might take several forms:

Discuss the political implications of the founding of the Federal Reserve Bank.

What was the economic effect of the founding of the Federal Reserve Bank?

What circumstances led to the founding of the Federal Reserve Bank?

Describe the legislative and other actions involved in the founding of the Federal Reserve Bank.

Formulate Questions on Topics and Answer Them

¹⁰ The purpose of this exercise is not to spot the specific questions that will be asked on the examination but to acquire further practice in thinking and expressing yourself clearly and cogently on appropriate topics. Especially at first, you will find that frequently you begin to answer a question and realize that you are off on the wrong foot, that you have not organized your answer well, or that you have not sifted out the pertinent facts and ideas from the mass of information you have about the subject. Answering an examination question is a more advanced phase of VERBALIZING. When you VERBALIZED a paragraph or a section in studying, you had immediately available all the facts to work with. When answering a thought-provoking question, you must select and pull together appropriate facts and ideas from your memory of a wide variety of paragraphs or sections or even chapters. With practice you will find yourself gradually becoming more fluent and skillful in formulating clear, pertinent, and comprehensive answers to the questions. It is much better to acquire this skill before entering the examination room than to try to develop it while taking the exam!

¹¹ This question-and-answer technique, by the way, is one of the best devices to use when several people are studying together. Let one person (rotating through the group) ask a question. Have everyone else take a moment to collect his thoughts on it, and then one person answer. Sometimes it is worthwhile for two or three people to answer the same question, to illustrate the different approaches that might be taken. With keen attention you can pick up good ideas from your colleagues not only as to the answer to the particular question, but on good form and procedure in answering questions generally. In short, from the question-and-answer technique, either alone or in a group, you can learn in two ways from each question: You can learn the answer to the specific question asked, and you can improve your ability to answer *any* question about material you know.

¹² It might be noted here that, generally speaking, the better the student, the less he has to gain from group study; conversely, the poorer the student, the more he has to gain from group study if, indeed, the group studies and does not allow the study session to degenerate into a mere social gathering.

Be in As Good Physical Condition As Possible

¹³ This involves nothing more than common sense applied to your own particular constitution and nature. It is merely sensible and reasonable not to show up for an examination groggy and yawning from lack of sleep, weak and irritable from too much coffee and too little food, stuffy or with a headache from not having stirred around and exercised, or logy and dopey from

overeating! Experimentation has demonstrated that having done a lot of mental work does not substantially affect people's mental efficiency—that is, your mind does not easily get tired to the point that you cannot think or remember well. However, related experiments have strongly indicated that a person in poor physical condition often simply does not have the energy, will power, or drive to put out the concentration and mental and physical effort necessary to do well on an examination. So do not be afraid of "tiring out your brain" in reviewing, but do be careful not to run yourself down physically to such a point that you lack the sheer physical energy and drive to endure the stresses and strains of examination week. When you sit up all night cramming, or even reviewing, it is likely to be not your brain but your body that is too tired to muster the concentrated attention and effort you need to think the next day. Moderation and common sense are the keynotes of this phase of reviewing.

14 As for pep pills and other pharmaceutical products that enable people to stay awake for extended periods of time—stay away from them! Although many students have incurred "nervous breakdowns" and fairly serious emotional disorders from the over-use of such products, this danger is not the primary reason for this advice. After all, the chances are good that you could take pep and stay-awake pills without having a nervous breakdown. The greater danger is this: no pills "give" you energy; they simply enable you to deplete your natural store of energy to an abnormally and dangerously low level. The inevitable letdown may come just when you need maximum alertness and mental clarity—about the time you begin the examination, for instance! This is all too likely to be disastrous to your academic success.

Powell has let final examinations slip up on him. He is carrying a standard course load of sixteen semester hours and is partially working his way through college on a half-time job as usher in a downtown theater. Thus far this semester he has maintained a middle-C average in all courses. He owes his passing average mostly to having taken good notes on lectures and to having a good memory of what was said in class, the combination of which enabled him to squeak by his monthly tests with passing marks.

Actually, Powell has studied the texts and other reading assignments relatively little—usually he has given them only one very fast read-through. Now it is suddenly the week before finals, and Powell realizes with dismay that he cannot rely on his memory of lectures and class discussions to get him through final examinations which will include all material covered in the courses, some of it as much as three or four months ago. It had not been too difficult for him to remember for only three or four weeks sufficient material for the monthly tests, but this is an entirely different proposition. Looking through the textbooks that finals will cover, Powell realizes that such scanty, marginal acquaintance with them as he has acquired during the semester has faded away to such an extent that most of the material seems only faintly familiar.

Three days are left in the school week, during which time he is supposed to work three hours each evening, and on Saturday he is supposed to work five hours. He has his final examination on French Monday morning, Tuesday afternoon he has American history, and has no exams scheduled for Wednesday. Thursday morning he has American literature, Thursday afternoon trigonometry, and Friday morning he has sociology. Based on his experience thus far, Powell figures that the trig exam will be the easiest for him and the history hardest. He decides to take a few minutes to try to chart a course of action that will give him the best possible chance of passing all courses.

1. Using what you have learned about effective study, schedule Powell's time in a manner that you think will give him maximum chance of passing all courses. You have three pre-exam school days, a weekend, and the final examination week to work with. As matters presently stand, Powell is due to work three hours each weekday and five hours on Saturday.

2. Having scheduled a crash study program for Powell, how would you suggest he go about studying history for the examination?

3. How might he most profitably proceed in reviewing French?

Taking Essay Examinations

15   There is more than a little art to taking an examination in which you express your ideas in your own words and at some length. Of course, the person who knows the subject best usually will make the best examination grade on that subject. However, it is definitely possible to gain, or lose, a few points on an examination strictly on the basis of certain skills that may have no relation at all to your knowledge of the subject. The remainder of this chapter explains a few examination room techniques, which may mean extra points for you. It does not go into such elementary things as having proper writing materials, extra pencils, and getting there on time, which college students should know without being told. Pay especial attention to the first four points in this section, as they are of unusual importance in taking an essay examination.

[16] There is no experienced instructor who cannot recall numerous instances when a student approached him after being handed back a graded test paper and asked, sometimes belligerently, "What's wrong with this answer?" And glancing at it, the instructor has said something like this: "The question asked for the social effects of the westward migration. You gave a nice description of the westward migration itself, but hardly touched on its social effects." The student thought a minute, looked surprised, and mumbled, "Ohhhh—I didn't think of that."

[17] Do not be in such a hurry to begin answering a question that you answer the *wrong one!* Use your common sense to identify the crucial words in a question, and take a minute to determine just what the particular combination of words means that you should do.

[18] Consider, for example, the question, "Discuss the social effects of the westward migration." First, "Discuss." This calls for more than merely listing, naming, identifying, or outlining. It might call for even more than describing, since "describe" rather limits the question to the social effects alone, while "discuss" implies that the answer might go into the social effects in terms of other political and economic phenomena of that period. Then, "social." You are not primarily concerned with the historical, political, or economic aspects, although these might be brought in through the breadth of the word "discuss." Primarily, the professor wants you to explore the *social* aspects of the migration, and not just any social aspects, but the *effects*. Depressions, immigrations, the Irish famine, all may have contributed to the westward migration and might be mentioned if you have time and want to weave them into your proper answer, but primarily you are not interested in causes in answering this question but in results, effects. What happened because of it? What changes did it produce? Finally, it is the "westward migration" you are to discuss the social effects of—not some other migration nor some other western phenomenon. Do not concentrate so hard on the Oklahoma land rush, or the Oregon Trail, or the building of the railroads that you limit yourself to discussing one aspect only of the westward migration. In other words, do not mentally substitute one element in the westward migration for the whole and write about the one element to the exclusion of the others. The experience of having formulated such questions and VERBALIZED the answers, as described previously, is invaluable in developing your skill in answering essay questions on an examination.

[19] One of the marks of a scholar in any field is his ability to handle the language of the field, think rationally in that area, and

Take a Moment to Outline Your Answer Before You Write

use logic as well as memory in solving problems in the field. Many teachers deliberately ask examination questions that require some acquaintance with the subject being studied even to understand the question, much less answer it! So do not impose upon yourself a penalty for carelessness—carelessness in perceiving what it is you are supposed to be answering. Analyzing a question by the process described here takes no more than thirty seconds. It can pay off handsomely in increased grades!

Outline the Answer to Each Question
Before Starting to Write

20   Have you ever been furiously writing away on the answer to some examination question and suddenly realized, with a sinking sensation, that although what you are writing is true enough, you have drifted far off the track? Have you ever, upon receiving your graded paper, looked over it and realized that you completely omitted one facet of an answer that you knew and had intended to include?

21   The best defense against such grade-lowering errors is to take a minute immediately after analyzing the question to jot down the major points you want to cover in your answer. Use a piece of scratch paper. Do not bother about complete sentences; simply list the things you think should be covered in your answer. Then check your list against the question to see if it really

covers the answer the question calls for. If it does, you are ready to begin writing your answer to the question. If it does not (assuming that you do have the necessary knowledge required for the answer), either your original analysis of the question was wrong or you drifted away from the import of your analysis as you thought out your outline of the answer. Whichever it was, you are far better off to discover your error now than you would have been had you spent the time necessary to write out a full answer to the question and only then, or even after receiving your graded paper back, found your error. It is bad enough to make a low grade on an examination because you did not learn the necessary material to answer the questions; it is absolutely maddening to *know* the necessary material and then make a low grade because you missed the cue and did not present that material! Outlining your answers before writing them can prevent this.

22   It should not take you more than a minute or two to outline most answers. You probably will find that spending this amount of time actually shortens the total amount of time required to answer any given question by eliminating the "head-scratching" time that usually occurs when you try to reduce your disorganized knowledge of an unanalyzed question into an intelligent answer.

23   There is also a bonus effect from this outlining step. An instructor is not merely interested in your memory of facts about the subject on which he is examining you. He is also interested in your ability to express these facts in a clear, understandable fashion. If you outline your answers before writing them, you can produce more coherent, readable answers, which will create a better impression in the mind of your instructor than would the very same information presented in a helter-skelter, haphazard manner. Think for a moment how much better a presentation you can give of an oral report that you have previously thought out and planned than of an impromptu, unplanned speech covering the same background of facts. You would not consider giving an important oral report without prior planning as to how you will present the relevant material. Similarly, you should not write unplanned answers on test or examination papers.

24   One of the necessary elements in mastering a subject is learning the proper relationships between different facets of the subject and how the different facts and ideas fit together—in short, how the material on the topic is organized. Outlining your answers permits you to shift the order and treatment of ideas into the best pattern before beginning the actual writing and lets you display your skill in giving the subject under question a systematic, logical treatment instead of recording a smattering of ill-related bits and pieces of information. There is

probably no professor alive who will not be more favorably impressed by such a well-ordered and well-organized set of answers than by equally correct answers so jumbled up that he must reread the paper two or three times to sort out the information and convince himself that it really is there—just cunningly concealed!

Answer Questions Fully

25 What constitutes a complete answer to a question is determined by the question itself and by the preference of individual professors. If the question specifies "Outline briefly," or "List the main issues in," or "Enumerate five," or other directions that show plainly that the instructor wants a bare tabulation, partial sentences and maximum brevity may be appropriate. Usually, however, your instructor will want you to discuss the points listed sufficiently to show that you understand them. From the number of questions on the examination and the amount of time you have, you can form a rough approximation of how fully the instructor wants the questions answered. Usually he expects you to spend all the time available; if you are a fast writer, you usually will profit from using that skill to give fuller answers than you would have been able to if you wrote more slowly.

26 Whether the examination consists of one question or twenty, you probably will make a better grade if you spend the whole allotted time in preparing your paper. There is, however, an exception to this rule: If you do not know enough about the questions to spend the entire examination period writing on them, stop when you have written all you know. The practice of attempting to hide ignorance under a mass of words on an examination is likely to hurt your grade. Any competent instructor can distinguish between a comprehensive discussion of a question and an attempt to fill up space with trivia to conceal a lack of knowledge. Being human, he resents attempts to mislead him, and is likely to give the bluffer no breaks in computing his grade. If you do not know much about a question, do not try to hide the fact under a snowstorm of words, but if you *do* know a lot about it, write as much about it as time permits. You have all to gain and nothing to lose!

Read Over Your Answers

27 You will be surprised at how frequently you can improve your examination paper by inserting a word, or making a note at the appropriate place asking the professor to turn to the back of the page for additional information, and elaborating there on a point you had omitted or passed over too lightly. An instructor understands that time does not permit you to rewrite the entire page to keep your paper neat and will not hold against you the fact that you keep trying to improve your answers. Check the grammar and spelling of your answers as well as their accuracy and completeness in this rereading. Although he may not actually mark you down for such errors, you may be sure that your instructor will form a lower opinion of your scholarship as a result of them, and this may unconsciously affect his computation of your grade. Resist, therefore, the temptation to write furiously right through to the last period of the last sentence of the last answer, and then with finality to say to yourself, "There! I'm through!" and straightway turn in your paper. Use whatever time remains to critically read your answers.

28   The foregoing suggestions are of primary importance in writing a good essay examination paper. The remainder of these guidelines to making the best possible grade on an essay examination are simple and obvious. Your attention is called to them here, but little explanation or elaboration is necessary.

Answer the Questions You Know First

29   First answer the questions you know, so the time you spend in racking your memory on harder questions will not keep you from doing your best on the questions you know well. Using a separate page for each question will permit you to do this and still keep questions in their proper order.

Write Legibly

30   Keep your paper as neat as you can, and write as clearly as you can, using one side of the paper only. Your instructor probably has a multitude of papers to grade. Anything you do to make his job easier will reflect credit on you.

Write Out Each Question

31   Unless told that this is unnecessary, write out each question. It saves a teacher's time and makes his job easier to have each question stated on each paper.

Count Your Questions and Answers to See That
None Is Omitted

32   This is especially necessary if you skipped around, answering questions out of order. While doing this, check to see that your questions and pages are all in the proper sequence.

An instructor has every right to resent a student's carelessness in arranging pages, requiring him to shuffle through them trying to guess the proper order. Number your pages.

Be Reasonable in Questions You Ask During the Exam

[33] A professor should be willing to answer pertinent questions that will not invalidate the examination as an instrument to measure your knowledge, and, if a test question is ambiguous, should be glad to interpret it. However, questions that attempt to pick answers to examination questions out of him, questions whose answers would give you an unfair advantage over others in the class, he will recognize and turn aside, and think less of you for asking.

[34] Of course, it is a good idea to study your individual instructors and try to determine their particular preferences and dislikes in examinations, just as you have done in all other spheres of work for them during the course. Study of the instructor can never substitute for study of the course material, but it can enable you to display what you have learned about the course in a manner that will be most appealing to him. He is using the examination as an instrument to estimate your knowledge of a subject. Anything you can do to present that knowledge in a manner that will increase his respect for your scholarship will help your grade.

Rachel is about to take the final examination on her chemistry course. She has a B average, has reviewed carefully for the exam, and feels confident she knows enough to do well on it. Her professor, however, is noted for giving essay examinations that require fast work to complete in the time allotted. Upon entering the examination room, Rachel is handed a mimeographed sheet with the questions on it. There are eleven, of which she is to answer ten. Upon careful inspection she decides that numbers 2, 5, and 9 will require fairly elaborate answers, and that the others can be answered somewhat more briefly. She thinks she can answer every question fairly well except, possibly, number 4. She takes a couple of minutes to decide upon a procedure which she believes will give her maximum chance of making a high grade, then starts writing.

Devise what you think would be the best strategy for Rachel to follow in taking this examination, utilizing the principles presented in this chapter and any of your own ideas that you think would help.

[35] Some students apparently hold the erroneous view that when taking what we commonly call an "objective" test, they are more or less victims of chance, that studying for such an examination is somewhat a matter of good luck if you hit upon something that appears on the test, bad luck if you do not. Despite some accusations of this sort, however, the best preparation for an essay examination is generally also the best preparation you can make for an objective examination. The process of getting ready for an examination, as described earlier in this chapter, is excellent preparation for either an objective or an essay test. You should review as much as possible, giving special attention to those things the professor stressed. It is good for you to formulate questions about important topics and think through the implications of them, even if you know you are to take an objective test. Certainly, it is equally important that you be in as good physical condition as possible.

[36] There are, however, some guidelines for you to follow in the process of taking an objective test or examination that will help ensure that you give the right answer if you truly know it. Following these guidelines has helped thousands of students improve their test scores.

Analyze the Question Before Starting to Answer It

[37] This is essentially the same analysis as in the case of an essay question. Look at the item (multiple-choice, true-false, short-answer, or whatever) and ask yourself, "What is the fundamental problem posed by this item? What is it really asking?" Look for the critical words that carry the thought of the item, just as you do in determining the import of an essay question.

Answer with Your First Impression, Then Pause and Reconsider

[38] Answer the question on the basis of your first impression, then pause to study your answer more fully to see if it really satisfied the question. When you get the question analyzed and really understand what it is asking, one answer probably pops up first and strongest in your mind. If it is a multiple-choice item, one alternative instantly appeals to you most. If it is a true-false item, your mind says, "That looks true (or false)." In the short-answer test, your mind just continues from the thought of the item to the fact or concept that rounds out the statement.

[39] Mark down the first answer that comes to your mind *after* you have analyzed the item. (This is different from marking down

the first answer that occurs to you when you glance at the item; it is the *first answer that occurs to you after you understand the real implication of the item.*) Then pause to reason the thing out a little further. Check the question again and review the different answers you might have given to see if, in the light of mature consideration, your first choice still looks best. If closer study of the possible answers shows that you clearly had overlooked a significant factor that definitely would change the answer, then change it; but if you are merely doubtful, not completely confident, trust your first impression.

40 Here is why this procedure will, in the long run, give you best results in taking an objective examination: If you definitely *know* the answer to an item, the chances are strong that the answer will pop into your mind first. If closer study proves beyond reasonable doubt that your first impression was erroneous—you *do* know the answer to the question but just slipped somehow— you change your answer and no harm is done. But haven't you sometimes looked at an item, at once seen the correct answer but then begun picking at shades of meanings in words, debating the possible hidden significance of a phrase, suspiciously scouting the possibility of a "trick" question designed to trap you into an obvious answer, which, by a technicality, was incorrect? So you teetered and tottered and swayed between one answer and another, and finally in blind desperation played "eeny, meeny, miney, mo" and stabbed at an answer. Such a system of answering minimizes your chances of getting the item correct.

41 If you *know* the answer, you will either get it on the first glance, or easily and positively correct yourself. If you are not sure that your answer is correct, remember this: Something made that answer look good to you at first glance. You may not be able to put your finger on just what it was, but *something* did. If you cannot identify a definite fact or idea that shows another answer to be better, the odds are definitely best for you to go by that first impression. It may have been a forgotten point made by your instructor which you almost, but not quite, consciously remember. It may have been something you read—you do not remember what, but it seems to fit in with this answer. Certainly you will miss some questions by following this rule, but not as many as you will by twisting and torturing the items and your mind, trying to read an obscure interpretation into them and then answering on the basis of the distorted meanings you have evolved.

Assume the Questions Are Straightforward, Not Tricks

42 Many students unnecessarily lower their grades on objective examinations by being suspicious. You can take it for granted that your professor will ask his questions as simply and directly as possible. He is interested in finding out what you know about the subject, not in measuring your skill at uncovering trick words or phrases. This is not to say that he never expects you to make fine discriminations, to know and allow for differences between standard terms in your field—*reflex* versus *instinct, federation* versus *confederation, sulphide* versus *sulphate, otocyst* versus *otoliths*, and the like. It means that he will try to make the meaning of his questions as clear as possible; he will try to avoid questions that have hidden meanings or that require meticulous reasoning just to get the import of the question. Many more points are lost on objective examinations through reading into questions subtle, hidden meanings that the professor never intended than are lost by failure to perceive a technicality that actually is there. So, read for obvious, straightforward meanings in the questions; do not distort their meanings looking for tricks, which are unlikely to be there!

Watch for Modifiers
That Affect the Meaning of the Question

43   Often the answer to a question will depend upon the *degree* specified in the question. The most common modifiers are words such as *all, always, most, some, no, not, except, unusually, sometimes, never, great, much, little, no more, equal, less.* Weigh such descriptive adjectives and adverbs in your analysis of the question containing them.

44   As a general, overall rule, remember that the instructor's purpose in giving an examination is to find out how much you know about the subject. It is not to measure your reading comprehension, not to produce an examination that no one in the class can pass, not to outguess you and ask things you never expected to be examined on. Keep these things in mind in deciding what to study most intensively in preparing for an examination, in reading and interpreting questions asked, and in formulating your answers.

After PREVIEWING this chapter, write your summary paragraph here.